JUNE 97

Dear Dad,
   If he writes a book with the same intensity as
playing baseball this should be good reading.
Happy Fathers Day

LOVE
Wayne Connie
& Kids

BOTTOM OF
THE NINTH

Written by Kirk Gibson
with Lynn Henning

SLEEPING BEAR PRESS　　　　**SLEEPING BEAR LTD.**
121 South Main　　　　　　　　7 Medallion Place
P.O. Box 20　　　　　　　Maidenhead, Berkshire
Chelsea, MI 48118　　　　　　　　England

Printed and bound in Canada by Friesen's, Altona, Manitoba.

10 9 8 7 6 5 4 3 2 1

Cataloging-in-Publication Data
　Gibson, Kirk.
　　Bottom of the ninth / written by Kirk Gibson with Lynn Henning
　　　p. cm.
　　ISBN 1-886947-13-9
　　1. Gibson, Kirk. 2. Baseball players – United States – Biography.
　　I. Henning, Lynn. II. Title.
　GB865.G515A3 1997
　796.357 092—dc21
　[B]　　　　　　　　　　　　　　　　　　　　　97-10162
　　　　　　　　　　　　　　　　　　　　　　　　CIP

ACKNOWLEDGMENTS

Saying thanks to all those who helped in some way in putting together this book would have required an additional chapter of text. So many people provided support, assistance and encouragement throughout the months that *Bottom of the Ninth* was in various stages of production.

To those who provided information and insights from Kirk Gibson's life and career, thanks first of all, to his parents, Bob and Barbara Gibson. Others who agreed to be interviewed include: Sparky Anderson, Bill Lajoie, Darryl Rogers, Charlie Baggett, Eddie Smith, Tom Smith, Mel Didier, Jerry Krause, Al Kaline, Mel Patterson, Alan Eskew, Sam McManis, Gordon Verrell, Gordon Edes, Jim Leyland and Alan Trammell. Their enthusiasm in talking about Kirk Gibson was as rewarding as the information they provided.

Thanks to those in publicity and sports information offices who researched facts and sent faxes that proved invaluable in clarifying what personal memory banks no longer could: Mike Davis of Major League Baseball; David Tuttle of the Los Angeles Dodgers; Connie Bell and Giovanni Loria of the Detroit Tigers; Jim Trdinich and Ben Bouma of the Pittsburgh Pirates; Ken Hoffman, Paulette Martis and Brian Tocco from Michigan State University.

Thanks to those who helped in unique ways to make this effort comfortable: to Cathy Gregg for her beautiful work in transcribing dozens of hours of tapes; to Jim Schaefer for some early editing assistance; to Sandy Kempa for always being cordial, professional, efficient and reliable—a wonderful person to call when in a pinch.

Thanks to Sleeping Bear Press, who proved throughout the wisdom and value of working with a premier book publisher. Sleeping Bear's craftsmanship and attention to people, as well as to a process, made this effort successful from the very beginning.

Thanks to JoAnn Gibson for her patience and graciousness as a long interview process took place, and thanks to Kirk Robert, Kevin and Cameron Gibson for being so polite and understanding when Dad was tied up with that guy and his tape recorder.

Thanks, most of all, to Kirk Gibson for agreeing to sit down and to talk about his life and his career. Contrary to what some people might think, it does not require an excessive ego to look back upon your life and turn those thoughts and memories over to a publisher. A good book on a worthy subject instead demands that a subject have a basic humility—a desire to share as opposed to a yearning for self-promotion.

Kirk Gibson was invited to do this book because of a feeling that many would enjoy and benefit from his unique life and experiences. His triumphs and mistakes will provide wonderful lessons for anyone pursuing a particular path in sports or in life.

As an athlete, he was always going to be worthy of book treatment. But it's as a man who has experienced so much from life's spectrum that Kirk Gibson serves an audience best. Thanks to him for the memories.

Lynn Henning

TABLE of CONTENTS

PREFACE

efeat the Beast. I thought for a while that it might be a good title for this book. Defeat the Beast is a theme that's central to every challenge, to every objective, I have taken on in life or in athletics.

The Beast, simply, represents the bad and the negative that is forever trying to triumph against an individual. I'm speaking about human forces when I talk about the need to defeat an internal Beast that lets us accept failure, that wants us to give up or give in, that urges us to take the easy way out and fall prey to weakness as opposed to seeing us prevail because of our inherent strength and character.

It's a lifelong battle to defeat that Beast. It confronts us in every facet of our lives. It has been my battle each and every day to get control over a force that has had me in its grip all too many times.

This book is about telling a world that, despite the fact that the Beast is forever with us, we can and must prevail against it.

I know, because I do. Time and time again I win. The loss column has a few marks on its side, yes, but it is coming back from those defeats that brings peace and happiness to my life.

As a kid growing up in the northern suburbs of Detroit, the Beast wanted me to be less regular about attending practices and games on days when I would have preferred doing other things. I had parents who helped me fight off those urges, and the sense of self-discipline that came from making a commitment was critical to my development.

The Beast wanted me to arrive at Michigan State as an anonymous freshman football recruit and to be content with at least one year sitting on the bench. The Beast wanted me throughout my college football career to give in to injuries, or to shy away from competitive challenges that might have been dangerous or risky. Instead, I was able to let the Beast know continually that I would be the boss and control my own destiny.

When an odd development occurred during my college days—an invitation in my junior year to join the Michigan State baseball team—I had every reason to agree with the Beast that I was involved in a stupid venture that was neither doing me nor anyone else a bit of good.

Instead, I got mad at the thought of surrendering, and thereby changed my life, radically and wonderfully, forever.

When I began a 17-year career playing professional baseball, the Beast became even more vicious and more powerful, and nearly emerged the winner. But during a number of dramatic periods and showdowns throughout my years in the major leagues, I won the biggest battles. In Detroit. In Los Angeles. In my personal life. The Beast had its moments, but Kirk Gibson had more of them.

This book is about all of the experiences, good and bad, during a life and career that I believe show that we can minimize the Beast's effects upon us. My life has been filled, and remains filled, with daily challenges. I must keep winning against a Beast that will never back down.

I want to share my stories from the battlefield, and from a life that has been blessed beyond comprehension. I hope these experiences will help any person with his or her battles in life, and against a Beast you will only overcome by calling upon your own personal levels of strength and determination.

Kirk Gibson

INTRODUCTION

My first glimpse of Kirk Gibson came on September 20, 1975, in the Michigan State football locker room following a game at Spartan Stadium. MSU had beaten Miami (Ohio), 14–13, and a freshman flanker, who had rockets for legs, had caught the pass that became the game's winning touchdown.

We were hoping for a few words from a kid no one knew much about that might help us write our game stories. Gibson, 18 years old and barely three months out of high school, stomped out of the shower and breezed past us.

"I'm not talking," he snapped. "You dogged us last week and I've got nothing to say."

Gibson was smoking over some things written a week earlier following MSU's loss to Ohio State, and rookie or not, he was going to let the media guys have it.

Looking back on that Saturday afternoon more than 20 years ago, three classic Gibson traits had emerged:

He had, rather dramatically, helped his team win a game.

He had also decided to unleash an opinion, no matter whom it rubbed wrong.

He was not a typical rookie.

The basis for this book is sparked, not only because of Gibson's exploits and knack for the dramatic spanning a couple of decades, but also because he has always had so much to say—whether you liked it or not.

Three years after his freshman debut, I became more aware of the complete Gibson package when I was covering Michigan State's football team for the *Lansing State Journal*.

He had a personality and style that were as one-of-a-kind as his athletic skills, which were stunning. I learned quickly that he was the best quote on the team. You could ask Gibson anything, about any subject, and get a response that was articulate and direct.

It became a battle not to stop by his locker. It was too tempting to lean on him to size up a game, to evaluate an opponent, or to explain why MSU's pass offense worked so well.

On top of that, he was 6-foot-3, 227 pounds, ran with world-class speed, and doubled as one of the meanest, orneriest, most fiercely loyal team players a team could ever have hoped to see.

A year later, he and I were both in Detroit—he in his first weeks with the Tigers, and I in my new position with the *Detroit News*. Over the next 16 years, spanning for each of us two separate stints with the Tigers and with the *News*, respectively, there were hundreds of conversations with Gibson that probably led to as many stories written about him.

He remained, on balance, one of the best thinkers and talkers I had encountered in sports. He had an intellect and a passion that made him unique. He never used a cliche. He did not waste words.

My experience was—granted—different from many who approached him. Other than that first episode in 1975, he never left me standing with an empty notebook when I had an assignment to speak with him.

I knew while he was at Michigan State that someday he would write a book. There was too much dimension to him, too much fire, athletically and personally, that would demand that he sit down and talk about the components to a life and to a career as unique as Gibson's.

I simply could not have known then the degree to which Kirk Gibson would influence Detroit and the sports world at large. I could never have imagined the glory he would experience any more than I could have foreseen the early years of despair. There was no real sense that he would generate so much controversy, nor any way to envision the Hollywood endings he would write for game upon game, spanning seasons and teams and sports.

We first talked about a book in 1979. I never again mentioned the idea to him until June of 1995. By December of that year, we had agreed that he should talk about his life and his career and those things from them that ought to be shared with an audience.

And sharing is really the idea behind *Bottom of the Ninth*. This is not a book that intends to glorify. Rather, this is a book about lessons, about discipline, about failure, about regret, about success, about courage, and about the kind of determination one rarely sees in sports, or in life.

Lynn Henning

CHAPTER *one*

I WAS THE NEXT MICKEY MANTLE, BUT SPARKY ANDERSON HAD DECIDED HE COULD DO WITHOUT ME. THE DETROIT TIGERS WOULD OPEN THEIR 1983 AMERICAN LEAGUE SEASON AT MINNESOTA, WITHOUT KIRK GIBSON. I WOULD BE ON THE BENCH, NOT GOOD ENOUGH IN MY MANAGER'S MIND TO BEAT OUT GLENN WILSON IN RIGHT FIELD OR JOHN WOCKENFUSS AS DESIGNATED HITTER.

Spring training had not persuaded Anderson that I could be relied upon. In fact, for much of the past year, our white-haired skipper had not been happy with me—as a baseball player or as a person. He had been patient enough with my injuries and on-the-field mishaps. But he knew he had a big problem with me, and he'd have to help me realize I had to change or there was no way I would make it as a professional athlete. I was on a downward spiral and very close to hitting rock bottom. He saw my best buddy, Tiger pitcher, Dave Rozema and me as a couple of jokers who were not taking seriously the business of playing major league baseball.

I learned of the lineup snub following a workout in the Metrodome a day before our opener. When I arrived at my locker in the visitors' clubhouse, knowing I would not be starting the next night against Twins left-hander Brad Havens, I was ready to explode on something, or somebody.

We were supposedly pennant contenders, and he was treating me, the superstar, to a seat in the dugout? I stomped through the clubhouse and into Anderson's office, and closed the door, aching to let him know what I thought of the insult.

"You ain't playin' tomorrow night," he said, digging into me. "You've been actin' like an idiot."

Taunts on top of a benching. I didn't need this. My anger was surging almost uncontrollably.

"What are you trying—"

"Young man," he said, cutting me off, his voice rising, "let me have a little talk with you. I've been around a long time. I've seen a lot of people with talent fall on their face, and you're heading there."

He could talk all he wanted, standing there, behind his gray metal desk. I wasn't listening to any of this crap. Not one more word. This embarrassment of Kirk Gibson was going to stop, and I was enraged enough at this moment to show Anderson that right here is where it would end.

I went for him, trying to pin him into the corner, ready to break him in half if necessary. I almost had him, and I swear I was going to bust him. But Sparky eluded my grasp, ran to the doorway, and turned.

"Gibson!" he barked, biting off his words, "One of these days you'll find out who the boss is around here, and it ain't you! You're going to have a nice seat next to me all year! *I'll pick* when you play!"

Too much time spent here in 1983.

"I DID WRONG HIM. YOU KNOW HOW YOU GET CAUGHT UP WITH THINGS. THE ONLY WAY I COULD COMPARE HIM TO ANYONE WAS TO COMPARE HIM TO MICKEY MANTLE, ALL BECAUSE OF THE TREMENDOUS SPEED AND POWER. BUT I SHOULD HAVE CLARIFIED IT. THERE WAS ONLY ONE MANTLE."

—*Sparky Anderson*

He disappeared into the clubhouse, leaving me standing in his office, alone, defeated, and humiliated. I was feeling low, and I was disgusted with everyone and everything.

I didn't know it at the time, but as I walked back to my locker, shaken and upset, I was bottoming out—as a baseball player and as a person. It had been a long time coming, and I could feel the disintegration taking place, on the day before the start of our '83 season. This would become the pivotal year of my life.

I had talent, but baseball was a difficult and unrelenting

game. I had potential, but everyone in the majors had expected me to be a baseball machine by now, a second coming of the legendary Mickey Mantle. Instead, I had dished out a healthy serving of injury and inconsistency during my 3½ years in the majors.

I compounded all the setbacks by being selfish and immature. I made life difficult for those around me. My image was becoming bad. I had a lot of bad habits. I was surly and demanding. I was unreasonable. I was fighting Sparky, the Tigers, the media, and the world at large. I knew it all. Or at least I thought I did.

I wanted to be a superstar, yet I wanted to be left alone by the public, failing to understand that it just doesn't work that way. I had lost the focus and determination that had been the trademarks of my early successes. I was not excelling. People would not leave me alone. They wanted to make me pay for the disappointment and resentment I had created among Detroit's baseball following.

What I found most frustrating about failing at baseball—what tormented me most during these tough years with the Tigers—is that I had brought all of this on myself. If I had remained a football player—as a first-round draft choice to the NFL out of Michigan State—I would have avoided many of the tangles and struggles that baseball dished out. Certainly pro football would also have forced me to grow up—something I wasn't quite ready to do—but this difficulty was compounded by the fact that baseball was hard for me.

Now, football—football I loved. It was easy for me, by comparison. In football I excelled, minus the grief and setbacks that were a natural part of a game as humbling as big-league baseball—the "game of failure," where failing 7 out of 10 times is considered a success.

One that didn't get away.

I had chosen baseball for seemingly sensible reasons. I could expect to enjoy a long career free from any major injuries, and, because of that longevity, I would be able to achieve greater financial security. I had made a commitment to baseball, knowing it would be harder than football. So I would suck it all up, no matter how inept I might appear.

On the field, it seemed the awful lessons of humiliation would never end. There were some awful hitting slumps (I was hitting .221 at the '83 All-Star break, and felt lucky to be doing that well), made worse by the fact that I could look *very* bad on particular at-bats. In the field, I butchered my share of fly balls, and often turned opponents' base hits into extra-base errors. Also, at that point my arm hadn't yet developed, so it wasn't as if I could compensate with one of those Al Kaline lasers from right field.

This 523-foot home run was big at the time, but it didn't win a World Series.

I GOT ALL THE BLAME. BUT THE ONLY THING I WAS GUILTY OF IN DETROIT WAS NOT LIVING UP TO EVERYBODY ELSE'S EXPECTATIONS. I GOT SLAPPED WITH THE MICKEY MANTLE THING RIGHT AWAY. I NEVER CARED ABOUT BEING MANTLE. I'M NOT MANTLE.

Early on I had savored, and agreed, with the Mickey Mantle comparisons. Now, they were haunting me. I still thought I was Mickey Mantle, but I wasn't even living up to an average ballplayer's standards—let alone Mantle's. In my mind, however, I wasn't the guy who had failed—it was everyone else who had failed.

This type of thinking did not help matters when, in the summer of 1983, still just a hodgepodge of a baseball player, I slugged a 523-foot home run against Boston that soared out of Tiger Stadium and landed on the roof of a nearby lumber company. This was actually the worst thing that could have happened. It generated even more publicity and attention, which made me think that by this one feat I had earned the right to play every day. But I wasn't hitting consistently, and I certainly did not hit that homer in the bottom of the ninth. It was a flash-in-the-pan sort of thing. Afterward I continued to struggle at the plate, and I was getting booed constantly.

I went into a 9-for-78 slump at one point, and it seemed as if everybody—Sparky Anderson, the fans, the newspapers, in fact just about all of Detroit—wanted me out of their sight. Gone. It appeared I was squandering my talent, especially after the potential shown by the monstrous home run vs. Boston, and it was too much for them. The tiring frequency of my injuries, topped by my surliness, had turned me into a negative presence.

But I was so cocky that I wouldn't admit I was headed for a crash landing.

Tiger's pitcher Dave Rozema and I became such notorious goof-offs that even something purely accidental, such as the night during spring training when I helped send him to the doctor for stitches, was viewed as one more embarrassment that, for the Tigers, made my erratic performance all the more grating.

The incident happened at a bar one evening during spring training, in Lakeland, Florida. Rozie had a cold sore and he had stuck a bottle of Camphophenique into his back pocket. There was only one chair for the two of us, and as he got ready to sit down, I yanked the chair toward me. It was fairly innocent, as behavior between buddies went—a high schooler stealing another guy's seat.

THE MEDIA

Early on, our relationship was rocky, and sometimes even volatile. I was over-matched by my surroundings and wasn't capable of dealing with the demands of interviews and autographs. I had never before had to accommodate people who weren't directly part of my team, therefore I displayed some brashness.

When I was preparing for a game, if you came for an interview that wasn't scheduled, I would tell you to get lost. Later, when I matured, and learned how to accommodate people and they knew to make an appointment for an interview, it would go much more smoothly. When they didn't respect where I was coming from—my mental preparation for a game, or winding down afterward—I was rude.

If someone wrote something unfair about me or my team, I would confront the writer. It was my job, and my teammates loved it. It was my personality. The writer expressed his opinion in what he wrote, and I was going to give him our opinion. In the end, I respected their obligation to do their job—both for the game and for the fans.

Rozie went down on his butt and the bottle smashed into pieces. He began bleeding from a gash in one of the worst possible places.

It made headlines, of course. Everything we did found its way into print, or onto the airwaves. We were regular fodder in the gossip columns, accused of everything and anything, including the purely fictional—like threatening a Greektown waitress with a gun. Through some fault of our own, we had become fair game for this treatment. The media were only too happy to report anything they heard, whether it was truth or myth.

I had incorporated into my life an all-time high of pleasures and diversions, which distracted me from my baseball development. I was totally self-centered, existing solely for the moment at hand. I even turned my back on my immediate family, in a way that is inconceivable to me today.

Thinking back on my mindset then makes me shiver now. It would be in the ninth inning, we would be getting beat, 8–1, in a game in which I had contributed absolutely nothing, and all I could think about was, "Let's get this thing over and get out of here."

Contrary to my upbringing, I showed no regard for others. Kids would be standing within my reach, begging for autographs, and too often they would get a harsh, "I'm not signing."

In spite of my behavior, the fans still supported me.

Long gone.

An out-of-town writer would approach me in the clubhouse, intimidated by my reputation, and just praying for a little civility. What he would get was a wave of my arm and a brusque, "I don't have time."

These and many other rude confrontations made people dislike me. But, in keeping with the backward way I was looking at things, I just didn't care.

To Sparky and the Tigers, my early '80s public relations problems were significant, but they were even worse combined with the fact that I was not becoming a dependable or productive major-league player. They had been patient with me, but by now I had lost my status as a special case with potential. They had originally planned that I would be a major offensive threat, a heart-of-the-order workhorse who could carry a ballclub. But I was just another part-time player, and playing so badly that I was being booed and harassed on and off the field.

By the end of the year, the beast had nearly defeated me. I was ready to quit. This is how bad things had become: I would be at home in the afternoon watching TV before a night game at home. At 3 p.m., a show would come on called *Good Afternoon Detroit*. This was my cue, my reminder, that it was almost time

Tiger Stadium at night.

to go to that dreaded stadium to once more face failure and humiliation. There was an ugly ache in my stomach, and I would feel myself coming close to tears. I didn't want the phone to ring because I did not have the spirit to speak to anyone. I hated my job, and I hated my life.

I had this sick feeling before every game. I felt everyone was against me. Every day I had to fight the urge to give up. All I wanted to do was escape each game, each experience, and the misery that was sure to follow.

Somehow I was able to make a strong finish in '83 to bump my season-ending average to a meager .227. I had only 91 base hits for the year. I was a part-time player who had generated more ink in the gossip columns than on the sports page, and there was talk—serious talk, even in the front office—that it might be time to ship me and my so-called potential to a different team and town.

At a time when the club was becoming a major contender, the Tigers could not afford to waste their efforts on a 26-year-old project who was embarrassing himself and his employers.

With that disturbing assessment hanging over my head, I spent all of October and November hunting. I needed this break from the pressure I had put on myself to do some serious soul searching. Sitting out in the woods by myself, my mind would start reeling. I couldn't run from myself, and all of my mistakes began to close in on me. The lies I had been living revealed themselves to me one by one. I was overwhelmed with how wrong my whole life was, but I didn't know where to turn for help.

Miserable and ashamed as Christmas neared, I was only a few days from an experience that would change my life.

Mr. Congeniality.

CHAPTER *two*

AN UNDISTINGUISHED TEENAGE ATHLETE GROWING UP IN

WATERFORD, MICHIGAN, I WAS BASICALLY A GOOD KID THANKS

TO TWO GREAT PARENTS AND A GOOD HOME. I GOT INTO A MIN-

IMUM OF TROUBLE GROWING UP, BUT I WAS PERFECTLY CAPABLE OF

DOING LITTLE STUPID THINGS, SUCH AS THE TIME I GOT CAUGHT STEALING A NEIGHBOR'S OUT-

DOOR CHRISTMAS LIGHTS. MY BUDDIES AND I WERE THROWING THEM UP IN THE AIR AND WATCHING

AS THE LIGHTS CRASHED AND POPPED ON THE PAVEMENT. QUITE A THRILL.

Until the owner of the house, who happened to be a good friend of my mom's and dad's, pulled up in his car, nabbing me in the act. He threw me in the backseat and drove away from the curb, very angry and stomping on the gas.

"I'm taking you right to the police station!" he yelled, really roaring at me.

My heart was pounding as we got to the parking lot of the police station, and terrible thoughts were running through my mind—like having to face my dad when he came to pick me up at the station. I mean, I was scared. Then the neighbor gave me the old, "Okay, I'm going to let you go this time. But you make sure you tell your dad what happened."

Of course, there was no way I could tell my dad. It would have been like requesting a firing squad. He ended up finding out from his friend, and I'm sure our neighbor was half laughing when he told him. My dad was pretty cool about it, although the message was clear that this kind of behavior was not to happen again. Ever.

Discipline, guidance, togetherness, love. Things were pretty simple in the Gibson household. I had two older sisters, Jackie and Teena, who were good athletes in their own right, and two parents who set the tone for a family that was all day, every day, into activities.

Softball. Baseball. Football. Basketball. Camping. Fishing. Snowmobiling. Skiing. And chores. We were always *doing* something. Led by my dad, Bob, and my mom, Barb, we were not a family to sit home and relax.

My dad, a tax auditor for the State of Michigan, and later a high school math instructor, was the single greatest coaching influence on my life and career. He was an intimidating, 6-foot, 205-pound man with a booming voice. He was my own personal drill sergeant. I never had a coach as relentless, or one as tough, and he had an intensity that would make you melt.

I'm sure part of his regimentation stemmed from the fact that he was a Depression child whose school years were spent trying to help his own family survive a miserable economic period that I can't even begin to comprehend. Even as a small boy, he was working, pulling a red wagon through the neighborhood, selling newspapers, or vegetables out of the family garden. It was a long way from the childhood I would know.

It was sad, too, that my father had had so few opportunities for competition, because he was very athletic and had great speed. As a kid, he forged his father's signature in order to play high school football. When his father found out, he forced my dad to quit. Later, the Navy provided him with a small opportunity to compete. He had served on the battleship Missouri as part of a taskforce that helped in the efforts to take Iwo Jima and Okinawa. After the war he played a lot of Armed Forces fast-pitch softball, a game he continued to play once he got home.

He was good enough and knowledgeable enough to coach kids' leagues in all sports. He also personally took charge of my development in football, basketball, and baseball.

It was my dad who taught me early on how to catch a football, and, more important, what to do with it after I caught it. "Take the ball and tuck it away," he would say. "Now, put your hand over the end." This training had a lot to do with the fact that I fumbled only once during my entire career at Michigan State.

My dad had a passion for mechanics, for fundamentals and details, which he would constantly drill into me. He also had a son who loved sports. A son who, while not the most talented kid on the block, had pretty decent size and growth patterns—stuff I had been displaying since birth. I weighed ten pounds, one ounce, and measured just under two feet in length, when they weighed and measured me inside the delivery room.

My mom actually remembers the doctor in charge half cracking up at my broad shoulders, and big feet and hands. At seven or eight months, without having gone through a crawling phase, my mom says I just stood up and began walking.

Later came the passion for running—one symptom of a kid who hated sitting still, who had to be doing something every minute. My parents took all my antics in stride, and focused on helping me develop through instruction and support. As I grew up, my dad, of course, drove me all year long, day and evening. Regardless of season. It was relentless to the point that I almost hated athletics because I couldn't get a break from it.

I'd be down the street playing with my buddies, and I'd hear this bellowing voice: "Kirrrk! C'mon, let's go! Let's get working!" And then we would begin our two-man practice and training sessions, concentrating always on technique.

During the school day, my dad would have lunch ready for me when I came home at noon, and outside we would go again, even in the middle of winter, when he would have me shoveling snow off the basketball court.

My dad went so far as to build a pitching mound and a home plate in the backyard, where we would spend countless

"WHEN I CAME HOME FROM THE HOSPITAL, I TRIED TO PUT HIM IN THE BASSINET AND HE WOULDN'T FIT."

—*Kirk's mother, Barbara*

summer evenings. He would be hunched down with his catcher's mitt, and I would be gunning from the mound, trying to find that elusive thing called a strike zone.

I'd get so ticked off at the baseball regimen that, every once in a while, I'd rifle a fastball off my dad's shins. He didn't care. He could see what I was accomplishing and how it would benefit me in the long run, even if he was pushing me mercilessly. I may have wanted to do other things and enjoy other experiences as a kid, but, because of my dad, they were all but out of the question. I was a full-time athlete.

I didn't realize until much later in life the lasting lessons of working to such excess. By paying attention to detail, allowing no mental mistakes, and gaining command over the things I could control, I would be able to stand a chance against someone of greater ability than myself. It was all part of knowing, as my dad knew, that my opponent would not be likely to go to the same lengths. In the process, he was preparing me for the biggest challenges that I would face in sports, as well as in life.

The Coats Funeral Home team (top right).

We did have some lighter moments, though. My dad was constantly challenging me to these impromptu sprints, even if we were just walking back to the car—and he was still fast.

"All right," he'd say with a snap, "Get set! Go!"

I won a few, he won a few, and we both enjoyed the sprints to the max, our own private dad-and-son competitions. We wrestled a lot, too. Just fun, binding guy stuff that I wish every son could experience and enjoy as much as I did with my dad.

My parents weren't at *most* of my games—they were at *every* game. No exceptions. It wasn't one of these deals where mom and dad live vicariously through a child athlete. Rather, it was two parents supporting their son, showing me that athletics could help a person understand discipline, humility, and risk and reward.

My mom, who was a speech and drama teacher, showed a different manner of dedication. She provided the foundation, and the love. I can still see her at every kids' baseball game I ever played in, wearing her sun hat and keeping a scorebook. Every game. Every year. But she helped to counter my dad and allow me some breathing room. Otherwise, I would have been practicing four times a day instead of two.

While my mom and dad were at every game and every practice, my mom was always there as the glue to hold the family together. As the only son, and the last born of three children, it was no surprise that while growing up I became a certified Momma's Boy. When times were tough, when a young boy was having his problems, I would invariably end up in mom's lap. Guaranteed.

BY PAYING ATTENTION TO DETAIL, ALLOWING NO MENTAL MISTAKES, AND GAINING COMMAND OVER THE THINGS I COULD CONTROL, I WOULD BE ABLE TO STAND A CHANCE AGAINST SOMEONE OF GREATER ATHLETIC ABILITY THAN MYSELF.

My parents weren't at most of my games—they were at every game.

Mom was calm. She was reassuring. She was my refuge against the never-ending regime of practice, practice, practice that I knew under my dad. And yet, she was no soft touch when I had gone over the line.

I remember when we were on vacation in Florida and I was at a stage where adolescence had instantly converted me into a 13-year-old adult. I was giving her some sass, and she finally had no choice but to give me a whack upside the head. I intercepted her arm at mid-slap and sort of snickered at her, real pleased that I had gained a certain equality in this relationship.

"Well," she said, this soft resignation in her voice, "You've finally grown up, I guess." Grinning, I turned to get into the backseat of the car, and she quickly gave me a hard kick in the pants that nearly lifted me off the ground. She was in my face, and I will never forget the words: "Don't you *ever* treat your mother like that again!"

She also helped balance a household, based around a schedule of three square meals, that was not always wrapped up in sports. Every summer we would go to Sugar Island, at the point where the Lake Superior and Lake Huron waterways connect, and for two weeks we would fish, swim, boat, pick blueberries, sit around the campfire—the works. Each summer, for 18 years, that was our vacation.

We had such a regimented life, and I noticed other kids and families enjoying less scheduled lives—a lot more pure leisure, you might call it. The goof-off in me envied that free-spiritedness, as I headed off to yet another practice or game.

Put that all together and you had a youngster who was more motivated by athletics than by the classroom, where I tried simply to get by with average grades. I do not look back on that as anything to be especially proud of, but my parents— and they were teachers, no less—understood that I wasn't lacking in intellect or character, but that my makeup wasn't cut out for excellence in a traditional classroom.

However, I did have a deep curiosity about things, and where curiosity and interest existed, I could be quite accomplished. Take nature, for instance. I was always down at the riverbank, looking for turtles, frogs, snakes, or whatever, and catching fish. I would take the fish home and fry them up—scales and all. I loved being near water and the wetlands chain-of-life. I found it enriching and instructive in a way that fascinated and awed me, and I wanted to understand all of the intricate parts of the environment. I still do today. I try my best to be environmentally sensitive, and I'm passing that philosophy on to my children.

What's surprising to most people is that I wasn't all that hot as a young athlete. In our high school I was among the good

> "HE IS A VERY PRIVATE PERSON. HE APPEARS ROUGH AND GRUFF, AND AT TIMES I DON'T LIKE HIM, BUT HE CAREFULLY PICKS HIS FRIENDS AND WOULD DO ANYTHING FOR THEM."
>
> —*Barbara Gibson*

I never lost a jump ball in four years of high school basketball.

players, for sure, but I was far from the best. (The best athlete was a guy named Bill Kurtz.) Any early distinctions had to do with—no shock—my size and my speed. I was a tall, skinny, big-boned guy who could run like the blazes, which gave me my biggest edge in youth football.

In high school, I was nothing extraordinary. I played junior varsity football as a sophomore, and progressed slowly as an athlete and as a football talent. I evolved from tight end to wide receiver, and then, in my senior year—because I wasn't getting the ball sufficiently as a wideout—I was turned into a running back and return man. At my new position I was good enough to eventually draw some college interest, though initially not from any Big Ten schools.

In basketball, skill-wise, I was an early version of Dennis Rodman. I could run, I could defend, and I had such an awesome vertical leap that never in four years did I lose a center jump. My problem was shooting. It might take me a couple of tries just to make a short jumper, and I was also pretty ragged on free throws.

In baseball, again, I was good but not spectacular. I never even played baseball my sophomore year because I got hurt just before practice started. It happened in gym class, during a square-off known as the Jocks vs. Freaks Wrestle-Around. This charming event consisted of guys issuing random one-on-one challenges to anyone who looked like competitive prey.

Since I was a Jock, and I had gained about 30 pounds during the summer before my sophomore year (it put me in the 165-pound range) a Freak who went about 230 challenged me to what he figured would be a one-sided beating.

I decided out of pure aggression to throw him as far as I could. When he came at me, I picked him up and slammed him down—squarely on top of my left hand, which fractured a knuckle. That quickly, spring baseball was eliminated.

With baseball out of the picture, I decided that, rather than just give up, I would implement Plan B. In this case, that meant I would go out for track instead. If a door closed on one option, I had been taught, you always had an opportunity to compete in something else. And a broken knuckle wouldn't interfere with my 880-yard relay times.

I definitely had some aptitude. That was established when we went to the Central Michigan Relays, one of Michigan's top high school track events. I was running the third leg on our 880-yard relay team. Almost no one there had seen me run before.

I took the baton—well behind the leaders—and then smoked everybody. There were people staring at me with "who's-that?" expressions on their faces, wondering where this gangly speedster had come from.

But it was in football where the headlines began showing up, especially during the fall of my senior year, when I scored five touchdowns and gained 311 yards in a game against Livonia Clarenceville. I finished the season with 734 yards on 95 carries, and I showed a lot of voltage as a kick returner. The previous year, I'd had a knockout game against West Bloomfield, scoring on a 67-yard pass play and a 75-yard kickoff return. Moments like these earned me Honorable Mention All-County as a junior and First Team as a senior. They also generated some impressive game-film footage that ultimately, albeit accidentally, won me a scholarship to Michigan State University.

Baseball, on the other hand, was more or less my summer hobby. And though I didn't like it as much as football, those summers during high school playing American Legion baseball for Waterford Chief Pontiac Post 377 were a lot of fun. We had quite a team, and I hit my share of home runs, including what might be called my first big bottom-of-the-ninth blast. It came during a zone championship game against Rochester at Portland, Michigan.

A victory would put us into the state tournament—pretty heavy stakes for a gang of teenagers, as we got ready for our last at-bat in a 1-1 game. We had a man on base, and I got to the plate with a chance to experience your basic 17-year-old's sports hero fantasy. I crushed one over the right-field fence to win the game. I remember dancing around the bases, revved and triumphant, just like I would after two crucial home runs I would later hit in professional ball.

Moments such as that should have left me filled with appreciation for the regimen my dad forced upon me for so many years. But it was a tough experience to overcome, the feeling of hating—absolutely hating—working at sports rather than playing at sports.

I guess the thing that made it palatable for me was that my folks refused to utilize sports as a day-care center. Never for a moment was it one of those deals where the parents may as well say: "We want to get you out of our hair for a few hours. Go play baseball."

Instead, they were there for me around-the-clock, on hand for everything I did, becoming in the process my eternal role models. I may have been a huge Al Kaline fan growing up, but I never confused an athletic hero with someone who would shape my life. My parents handled that. Every single day. They were, and still are, my heroes.

American Legion State Champions, 1975 (top row, second from right).

CHAPTER *three*

FOR A LIGHTLY RECRUITED, ALL-COUNTY WIDE RECEIVER FROM WATERFORD, MICHIGAN TO HAVE A CHANCE OF BEING IN MICHIGAN STATE UNIVERSITY'S FOOTBALL PROGRAM, I HAD TO DO SOMETHING DARING OR DRAMATIC. THAT WAS AT LEAST ONE ASPECT OF AN 18-YEAR-OLD'S AWARENESS THAT WAS SURPRISINGLY ADULT AS I GOT READY FOR MY FRESHMAN YEAR AT MICHIGAN STATE.

I doubt if Michigan State recruited any lesser-known high school football players during the winter of 1974–75. None of the big schools had so much as sent me a letter. Dartmouth had written to me, and I was being recruited by a couple of Mid-American Conference programs: Central Michigan and Eastern Michigan.

Central was going to be my ticket, until the phone rang one Saturday morning in January while I was at home cooking an omelet.

"Kirk, this is Andy MacDonald from Michigan State. I saw you playing football on film. Last week I watched you play basketball against West Bloomfield. Thought we'd invite you up for a visit. You're a good one. Do you like Michigan State?"

I hadn't known anyone from State was even looking at me. I came to learn that MacDonald, who was an assistant coach to Denny Stolz, had noticed me by accident as he was sizing up some star from West Bloomfield High School. When MacDonald did check me out, it was during a basketball game. He had liked my size, the way I ran and jumped, and, I guess, my aggressive play.

MacDonald was right to the point when we spoke. I liked that. I was pumped.

"Yeah, I love it up there," I said. "My mom grew up in East Lansing and graduated from MSU." The following Saturday morning I was on my way to Michigan State to meet the head coach, Denny Stolz, and to learn about life at a Big Ten university.

Everything on campus was so big, so impressive—like a dream I was actually living. I remember walking into Spartan Stadium with Coach Stolz and some other recruits, stepping onto the field and saying to myself, "Man, I'd give anything to play here." It was overwhelming.

That Saturday night in East Lansing sealed it. The coaches took us to the Pretzel Bell for dinner, and then the older players showed us around East Lansing and its night spots. It was incredible seeing and being part of all the excitement the football team generated. That was the finest night a high school senior could have enjoyed, living or dreaming.

It still felt like a dream the next morning when Stolz called me into his office at Jenison Field House. There were rumors that Michigan State might be in trouble with the NCAA, but I really didn't care. MSU was the only major college that had talked to me, and Stolz impressed

Press Day, 1975.

me. He was low-key. He looked like a football coach. And he got straight to business.

"Kirk," he said, "it's very probable that we're going to offer you a scholarship to enroll at Michigan State. We have to see who commits and who doesn't, but we want you in the Spartan football program."

I didn't commit on the spot, but I knew where I wanted to play. And it wasn't at the University of Michigan, which had pretty much ignored me.

A few days after my East Lansing visit, Bill McCartney—Bo Schembechler's top assistant at the University of Michigan, who a few years later left for Colorado—called the house to say they had experienced some changes on staff, that they hadn't meant to be so long in contacting me, that they'd like to stay in touch and....Well, what happened is that Elliott Uzelac, another of Schembechler's assistants who had seen me as a junior and been impressed, became the new coach at Western Michigan.

When Uzelac left, recruiting assignments changed, and that was one reason there had been no followups. I hadn't been home when McCartney called, but it wouldn't have mattered anyway. I respected what Bo Schembechler had done in Ann Arbor, but I had no interest in playing football at Michigan.

With absolutely no fanfare, I signed with Michigan State in February, the first day tenders could be accepted. In fact, I was a late addition, and was only offered a scholarship because some other big-name recruits had turned them down. I was now part of a recruiting class brimming with All-Staters and All-Americans who made my high school accomplishments look feeble by comparison. The other recruits might have won the awards, but that just motivated me to work harder. I was determined to win a starting job for our first game against Ohio State University on national TV, though in everyone else's mind that would never happen.

I decided months before reporting to Michigan State that I would make a major impact on the team. And I had a plan in mind to reach that goal. I focused first on conditioning. The coaches were going to see a whole new level of physical stamina and mental toughness, which would show how willing I was to sacrifice. When the hotshots were running plays and conditioning drills with their tongues hanging out, I would be going at extra-high horsepower.

So, Greg Ruggles, a high school friend, and I set out on a summer's equivalent of Marine Corps basic training. Five or six mornings a week—through June, July, and August—we ran. We would go over to Kettering High School's track for a series of sprints that would set our legs and lungs on fire.

We'd run the gamut, starting with an 880-yard warm-up. Then, down the scale: 440s, 220s, 110s, 60s, 40s, 20s, as hard as we could run, on ugly cinders, to the point of absolute exhaustion. I'd take a quick rest, and then push it again to total exhaustion. It was as much mental as it was physical. I knew that if I could perform on the football field when the others were fatigued, or if I could run better while fatigued than they could, I would excel against them. It would give me an edge, regardless of the other guys' abilities or reputations.

Conditioning was only the first part of the plan. The second part was to show the coaches I was tough, and the way to do

> **I SIMPLY DECIDED THAT I WOULD BE THE FASTEST, THE BEST-CONDITIONED, THE HARDEST-HITTING, AND THE MENTALLY TOUGHEST PLAYER I COULD BE. THEN WE'D SEE HOW, OR IF, I MEASURED UP.**

that was to stick somebody, and stick 'em good. I would pick out the baddest sonofabitch on defense and hit him like a freight train. It might be suicide for a punk rookie to behave so arrogantly, but I had set my goals high. I wasn't going to just take it slow and get a feel for big-time college football—I was going to be a part of big-time college football.

I had no idea who, or how good, my competition really was. There was no way of knowing, no matter how fast I was becoming, if it would be fast enough to compete against Michigan State's existing or incoming talent. I had no sense for how hard players on that level hit, or if my best hits were enough to make a dent against that level of athlete. I simply decided that I would be the fastest, the best-conditioned, the hardest-hitting, and the mentally toughest player I could be. Then we'd see how, or if, I measured up.

I reported for camp in mid-August, and instantly reality set in when I realized that Mom and Dad weren't there. I was struck by the enormity of the campus, the 76,000-seat stadium, the huge buildings everywhere. I felt homesick, and I was completely out of my comfort zone. Worse, there were no students on campus yet, other than football players. It was August, it was hot, and I was lonely.

It didn't help that the schedule was so punishing. They got us up each morning, barely past dawn, for breakfast followed by team meetings. Then it was over to the stadium to get taped. We'd go through a couple of hours of grueling practice, running and hitting all morning, have the tape stripped from our skin (which burned so bad because a layer of skin was coming off with the tape), take a shower, then drag ourselves back to Case Hall for lunch. This was followed by a whopping rest that, on a good day, would last all of 30 minutes. Then it was back to the stadium to re-tape, all before we headed back out to run and hit all afternoon.

At the end of afternoon drills we'd get to re-peel that miserable tape again. It wasn't much fun, but then that's college football during two-a-days. After practice and a shower, we'd have dinner at the dorm, followed by more team meetings, at which time the coaches would cheerily tell us we had a whole hour before our customary pre-bed snack, followed by lights out.

We'd haul our sore, tired bodies back to our rooms for an hour, stagger downstairs for a piece of fruit or some ice cream, then sleepwalk back to our rooms, where we would collapse —physically and mentally.

It was boot camp, with recruits from all walks of life. I found myself putting on football equipment alongside guys from California, Ohio, Oklahoma, Texas, Colorado. White, African-

American, Hispanic. From big cities and from small towns.

Talk about being out of a comfort zone. I was now with people I had formed preconceptions of before even meeting them —but I had to put those preconceptions aside, because they were my teammates and we had to coexist in order to succeed. Before long, I realized that, though culturally we were all different, in a larger sense we were actually very much alike.

I'm not only talking race here. I discovered that the white guys from Pittsburgh and from Warren, Ohio were as different from me and my background as were the black guys. Everybody had a different story, different influences. But the commonalities—family, high school, girl problems, adolescence, football— put everyone on the same plane. I learned that prejudging people just doesn't work in the real world. As the days passed, I began to find this wild mix of people and styles less of a threat, and more of a kick.

Another big shock was my first visit to the football weight room, which was then located inside the Men's Intramural Building next to Spartan Stadium. The experience was pretty deflating. I wasn't a big weight lifter, so my first time there all I saw were guys from the team throwing 225 pounds on the bar and pumping it up and down as if it were cotton candy. I couldn't even dead-lift 225 pounds. I immediately realized I had to prepare further, and lifting would become part of that preparation.

I had been making an impression at practice, though, thanks to my speed and my summer conditioning, and I was really beginning to feel good about myself. They had a basic wind sprint drill where everybody lined up at the 50 and thundered to the 10. For me, *everything* was a competition, and I'd lead the first one, the second one, the third one, and the fourth, trying to finish in front every time.

I could be dead tired, but when they blew the whistle I was roaring all the way to the chalk. I established right then and there that I wasn't playing for second place—even in practice.

Of course, what pleased the coaches didn't always please some of my teammates, particularly the upperclassmen, who resented a rookie outracing them. It was that way in PTs (power training), where the team is broken into groups according to players' speed. My group was the fastest group— quarterbacks, running backs, receivers, and defensive backs.

Each unit would be stationed at a corner of the field. When the whistle blew, two groups at diagonal corners would take off on a dead run while the other two groups would get rolling on a round of gut-busting calisthenics: push-ups, sit-ups, leg-lifts, whatever. Then, arriving back at our corner, it was our turn to dive into the cals while the other two groups would sprint a quarter of a mile around the field. It was a slice of hell. The first day we ran PTs I led all six rounds. And that's when I started hearing it from some of my cohorts: "Hey, rook, you better slow down. These are hard, man." I just shook my head and kept running full-steam. I wasn't just leading the pack, I was considerably out in front. On the second day I did it again, and on the third day I was informed in no uncertain terms that the Olympic stuff had to stop.

It went from, "Hey, you wanna take it easy on these things, 'cause they're hard," to, "Hey, enough's enough. You're showing us up, Gibson. Now slow down!" At which point I just got up and took off again and beat 'em all back to the station.

The atmosphere became edgy. When the whistle blew for the next run, the guys in my group tried hemming me in with an on-the-run human barrier to slow me down. I just lowered my helmet and bulldozed through as a few of the guys worked me over with punches, and as I passed them I looked back and yelled, "Bye!"

I sprinted around the field. Just sprinted. I beat them so ridiculously that I was back at my spot in the southeast corner of Spartan Stadium before the rest had even gotten halfway across to the opposite-side 50-yard line. Everybody in the place saw it. I was not going to be denied by anyone.

Still, for all the pace-car stuff I was pulling in those first days of practice, nobody was saying anything significant to me. Not coaches, not players. There might have been a guy or two thinking, "This guy's psycho," but nobody said it. I got zero feedback. That's the way it works with freshmen.

My attitude was different from that of other freshmen—I expected to start, and I refused to go along with the upper-classmen's hazings. There was a ritual where freshmen had to stand at dinner, in front of the entire team and coaching staff, and sing their high school fight song. I never did. When the elders told me to sing, I told them I didn't care what they did to me, "I'm here to play football, not sing. I'll make my sacrifices on the field." I had made it clear from the start that I didn't play that game, and they sensed an intensity about me that said, "Don't push him."

The message that I would sacrifice my body for the team was reinforced at our first full-blown Saturday scrimmage. I had been waiting for this opportunity, and when they called for a crackback block, it was time. I had shown them I could run, but if I was going to start, they needed to know I could hit like the second coming of Dick Butkus. And the only way to get that point across was to take on the guy everyone

Tommy Graves.

acknowledged as the fiercest man on the field. That, without question, was strong safety Tommy Graves.

He was 6-3 and 211 pounds, fast, tough, and a hitter the likes of which even State's older coaches had never seen. Nobody messed with Tommy Graves. Which was exactly why I planned on knocking his butt into the tuba section.

I was on second team offense at the time, which meant we were going against first team defense. I hadn't been on the field for more than a minute when the quarterback, Charlie Baggett, called a sweep where I was supposed to crackback on the strong safety, who I knew was Graves.

I vividly remember going after Graves amid those flying bodies, cutting back at full speed and hammering him with everything I had. He never saw me coming. It was a tremendous collision. I had both chin straps on my helmet buckled in preparation, and I absolutely flattened the meanest SOB wearing a Michigan State uniform in 1975. No one on the field could believe it—especially the coaches, because they quickly called the same play again. The first hit didn't fully prove what I was made of. The second *would.* This time Graves was waiting for me. Through his face mask I could see an expression that said, clearly, "Bring it on." My brain told me, "Don't do it." Graves had been laid out by a *freshman,* and he was ready to tear my head off and re-establish why *he* was the baddest.

I cut back across the field, aimed squarely for Graves, and this time it was like a couple of bighorn sheep smashing heads. The sound of the collision was awesome—it was heard clear up in the stands. Neither one of us got knocked out, but we both felt like we'd been hit by lightning. I slowly walked away, my breath gone, my shoulder numb, not letting on that I was stunned and groggy. Now there was no question: the coaches knew I would sacrifice for this team.

The day after the Graves showdown, we were in a team meeting going over films when they put up the depth charts and announced I was starting at flanker. Mission accomplished. I handled the news with great dignity and maturity. I went straight to a pay phone in Case Hall and called home—"Mom, Dad, I'm starting!"

No holding back, no need for playing it cool. Winning a starting job as a freshman was my personal triumph over all the homesickness, the loneliness, the exhaustion, and all the adjustments in making the transition to big-time college football.

In our opener on national television vs. Ohio State, one of the most heavily hyped games in MSU history, we lost, 21–0. I had played like a freshman on a horribly deflating day in East Lansing, although, in one sense, I learned things in our dud performance that probably made me a better player later on. But I felt pretty overwhelmed going back to the dorm that night.

I realized the learning process had to continue. For a kid trying to get a handle on college football's complexities, each day was like climbing against an avalanche. Learning how to block, when to block, what pattern to run, when to turn left, when to turn right, when to go long, when to go short, how to make reads—it was staggering.

Because I was a freshman, when I messed up I was reamed by my receivers coach, Jimmy Raye, who had this high-pitched, screaming falsetto I can still hear:

"KIRRRK GIBSONNNN! KIRRRK GIBSONNNN! DAMMIT, KIRRRK GIBSONNN!"

It was the way coaches communicated with a freshman, especially one they had entrusted with a starter's role. There would be no mercy. Nor any from a veteran quarterback, which is what we had in Charlie Baggett, a three-year starter.

He and I had our first confrontation a month into the season, during a game at Notre Dame that we ended up winning, 10–3. It happened following a play where I was supposed to go downfield 15 yards and, depending on how far off the defensive back was playing, either go long or hook up for a pass beneath the coverage.

The defensive back was playing well off me, so I button-hooked. Baggett threw long, and the ball was intercepted. Now, coming onto the sideline, they were all over me.

"Hey," I said, "I did the right thing. He was off me, the play was to hook up—"

"Awww, bull!" Baggett shot back.

He and the coaches put the blame on me right there and then. All of it. I had no choice but to sit and take it with my mouth shut.

Some vindication came the next day, inside the locker room at Spartan Stadium, when we met to go over game films. We watched the play, and it was clear Baggett had made the wrong choice. It was just as obvious that I would not be getting any apologies from him, nor from Jimmy Raye, even if everyone in the room knew who had screwed up.

They could not show up Baggett, not when a freshman stood to gain stature at the expense of a team's senior quarterback. Never. However, Andy MacDonald, who had recruited me and was our offensive coordinator and quarterbacks coach, did sort of clear his throat and say, "Well, Charlie, guess you kind of overthrew that one."

A week after the OSU debacle I scored my first touchdown as a Spartan—the game-winner—on a 56-yard pass from Baggett, as we came from behind to nip Miami (Ohio), 14–13, and halt its 25-game winning streak.

I had shown some big-play potential, although getting the ball was going to be tough when MSU's offense was so rigid. It was classic down-and-dirty Big Ten football, 1975 style. Blocking, running, defense. Woody Hayes, Bo Schembechler, Denny Stolz football. Three yards and a cloud of dust.

I caught all of nine passes for the season, good for four touchdowns, all during an up-and-down fall that saw us finish 7–4. There had been some crazy moments to accompany the physical and psychological bumps and bruises. It was a typical freshman starter's initiation to the big show.

My favorite pattern—an 18 yard crossing route.

I remember our season finale vs. Iowa, at Iowa City—a miserable November day made worse by Kinnick Stadium's field, which was frozen solid. To get the turf to thaw they applied salt, which burned like fire as it leeched into the cuts and scrapes a player picked up along the way.

At one point in the second quarter, I went to block a Hawkeyes defensive back, who forearmed me across the face mask just as my chin strap came unbuckled. The bridge of my helmet slammed down on my nose, which cracked like a piece of plywood. I stayed in, but the pain was horrendous and I couldn't wait to get inside the locker room at halftime.

The trainers got me up on a table and looked it all over. "Uh, yeah, no question, you've broken your nose," they announced. Then one of them hollered to Troy Hickman, who was our assistant equipment manager: "Hey, Troy! Get Gibson a new double chin strap!"

Here I was hallucinating from the excruciating pain, and the solution was, "Get him a new strap and hopefully this nasty thing won't happen again." I laugh about it now. At the time, though my eyes were watering from the pain, I realized it was just part of the sacrifice.

I did score that day on an 82-yard bomb from Baggett, as we beat Iowa, 27–23. That touchdown said everything about my 3½ month initiation to big-time football. Though it spoke of my ability, and, most of all, my potential, I knew we would have to work that much harder in the off-season to get to our ultimate goal—the Rose Bowl.

But our Rose Bowl dreams suddenly received a crushing blow. The NCAA declared in January after my first year that MSU was being placed on three years of probation for recruiting violations. Stolz was fired, and our goal was shattered, never to be reached.

CHAPTER *four*

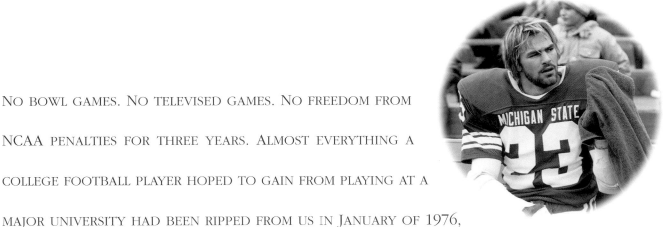

NO BOWL GAMES. NO TELEVISED GAMES. NO FREEDOM FROM NCAA PENALTIES FOR THREE YEARS. ALMOST EVERYTHING A COLLEGE FOOTBALL PLAYER HOPED TO GAIN FROM PLAYING AT A MAJOR UNIVERSITY HAD BEEN RIPPED FROM US IN JANUARY OF 1976, WHEN THE NCAA SOCKED MICHIGAN STATE WITH PROBATION BECAUSE OF RECRUITING VIOLATIONS.

The response from many was predictable—quit, find a new team, transfer. Because we didn't have a coach, there was no focus on a winter conditioning program. Then, in April, the announcement came: Our new head football coach was a guy from San Jose State by the name of Darryl Rogers.

"Darryl who?" we all wondered. They said he threw the football like crazy, which instantly got my attention, after having caught only nine passes as a freshman. When Rogers first came to speak he was definitely different, and obviously Californian. On one hand, he was strong and direct, as when he told us, "I'm here to win football games." But where a guy like Stolz had this serious, poised, above-it-all air, Rogers was real down-to-earth, and he talked in this kind of voice-through-a-pipe tenor that, at times, made him sound like Kermit the Frog.

What I could not have known in the first days of that season was this: Darryl Rogers would change my life, dramatically and permanently. The first change: we were going to air out the football.

At spring practice, Rogers was already re-tooling the offense top to bottom. First came a new quarterback, Eddie Smith, a skinny six-footer who was going absolutely nowhere in the Stolz system. Smith could do one thing and one thing only—throw a football the way some guys throw darts. He had finished first team All-State in Pennsylvania—beating out future NFL star Joe Montana.

Rogers took one look at that high, quick release, at the way Smith zipped passes down-field, and on the spot made him our starting quarterback ahead of three other guys. With me, though, he wasn't so sure. Darryl had actually wanted to make me an outside linebacker, figuring that was the best way to get the most production from a sophomore with my size and mobility.

But once Mr. Offense got a gander at our team speed—or lack thereof—he decided I'd better stick at wide receiver and help get us some points. We were going to need them in the fall of 1976. Things were still a mess following the probation upheaval, and the results of our disintegrated winter conditioning program left us weaker and slower than any of the Big Ten contenders.

Rogers may not have experienced Big Ten football before, but he was coach enough to understand that we were in trouble. He also understood that throwing the football was one way a weaker team could compete, especially when so many of our best players were on offense.

In the opener against Woody Hayes at Columbus we were bombed, 49–21. I caught a couple of touchdown passes, one of them for 82 yards. A couple of weeks later I caught five passes for 173 yards, which at the time set a MSU single-game record for reception yardage, and we tied North Carolina State, 31–31. I ended up leading the Big Ten in receiving with 748 yards on 39 receptions—30 more than in my freshman year—during a season which saw us finish 4–6–1, mostly because other teams ran over us, or past us.

I separated my shoulder in the season finale, at home, against Iowa. It happened just before the half. Eddie Smith was scrambling for his life, so I came back to help out, breaking off from the coverage and grabbing a pass a second before he would have been chewed up by the pass rush. I was zigging and zagging with the ball—anything for a few extra yards—when this linebacker the size of a pop machine blindsided me square in the shoulder, knocking me backward at least seven yards.

He stood over me doing this boxing referee countdown, "One, two, three!" which made me so hot that I forced myself to stagger to my feet. We exchanged pleasantries for a moment or two, and then I hobbled off, looking at the clock as I went. I remember being grateful there were only 27 seconds remaining until the half. When I got inside the locker room, State's doctors

Touchdown MSU!

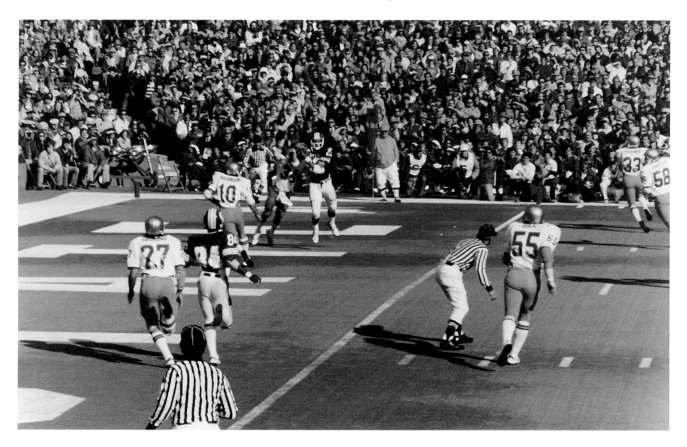

right away informed me I had an acute separation of the shoulder—which I'm sure I could have confirmed on my own. The pain was so strong I couldn't lift my arm.

"Basically, we can do one of two things," they told me. "We can block it out (give me a pain-killing injection), or just go with it." Not for a moment did I or anyone else suggest I might be out of the game. It wouldn't be my final incident in an Iowa–MSU matchup.

Chalk up another lesson in sacrifice, driven by the psychology of mind over matter, as I wasn't taking any injections in the shoulder with a 4-inch needle. So I ran the whole half with my shoulder tucked in protectively. I might as well have stitched a bulls-eye to my jersey. Every time we ran a play, the lovable Hawkeyes made sure to pile on and grind the shoulder extra hard.

As Iowa was our last game, and with no bowl games to go to, I had the off-season to let my shoulder heal. The coaching staff, though, wasn't about to let up on us. To combat our serious deficiency in strength and speed, on came a winter carnival known as the Be-At-Jenison-At-8 a.m. conditioning program. It was headed up by our offensive line coach—and former Green Beret lieutenant—C.T. Hewgley. Each morning, after we had gotten up and walked across the dark frozen campus and on into Jenison Field House, we could look forward to Hewgley bellowing at us as we sweated and steamed around the indoor track.

We'd begin with stretching exercises, then he'd have us jumping over these tall boxes, then on into sprints—220s, 110s, 60s, and 40-yard sprints. He punished us all winter long. Hewgley's drills were irresistible to me. I turned every sprint into a race, and my teammates picked up the challenge.

You could see what was now happening with our entire football team. We were getting back our character, our speed, our muscle, our purpose. It was becoming *our* team. The greatest challenge to the coaching staff and to the players was fighting through that first year of probation and working hard in the off-season to re-develop the total team concept. We had to set new goals now that the prospect of a Rose Bowl had been taken away.

We were also responding to the Rogers offense, which was very innovative by college standards. By the start of our '77 season he was placing more and more trust in Eddie Smith to run the offense with greater freedom at the line of scrimmage.

Soon all of us were able to read defenses and react to them. Smith was calling audibles at the line, and the receivers were changing routes on the fly. *We* were now the aggressors. It was very complicated, but the genius of Rogers was that he had a terrific way of making it sound so simple:

"It's no big deal," he'd say, kind of spreading his hands, palms up, and shaking his head. "If they go right, you go left. They go deep, you go short."

The guy could coach. And practices were interesting. Very NFL in nature. The air horn would sound, right on schedule, and we would move from one drill to another, always working on the pass offense. All day, every day.

By the start of my junior season I had come a long way from being a skinny high school first-team All-County. When I arrived on campus in '75 I was 188 pounds, and I finished the season at 198. My sophomore year I was 208, then 218 as a junior. By the time I came back for my senior season, I was at 227. Even better, my 40-yard times had gone the opposite direction each year: 4.6, 4.5, 4.4, 4.3, and even a split-second lower.

Size and speed were great, but they still didn't stop me from getting "cut" during our home opener against Purdue. I caught a ball deep in Purdue's end of the field and began churning upfield, running over a couple of defenders on my way to the end zone. That's when a defensive back torpedoed me with his helmet, right on the side of my shin bone. It was the first time I had ever been "cut," and I went flying. I hurt for three weeks.

Ray Greene, our receivers coach, who had worked in the old World Football League, a few nights later taught me a little maneuver known as "The Flipper," which was designed to put the cut artists out of business.

I would take the ball while running and cradle it in the arm opposite the defender's side. If he were coming low, helmet first, I would get down just as low to intercept him, discreetly submarining my fist into either his solar plexus, beneath his shoulder pads, or square into his Adam's apple, which would leave him gasping for air.

While trying for the next 10 minutes to find his breath, he could contemplate the wisdom of plowing his helmet into a man's lower leg. It was purely a survival tactic—one that ensured that if a tackler tried to cut me, he would pay for it.

 Football is an intimidating sport, and you absolutely *must* be the intimidator. When I looked across that line of scrimmage, I knew I had to own the defender, physically and mentally, because when you've defeated him both ways, you have an edge. I call it the mental press.

The Flipper was just a new addition to my overall strategy: I wanted to punish a tackler, not illegally or unethically, but to the point where he would close his eyes. If I could get a tackler to close his eyes—believe it, most players close their eyes at contact—then I could make him miss, and outrun him.

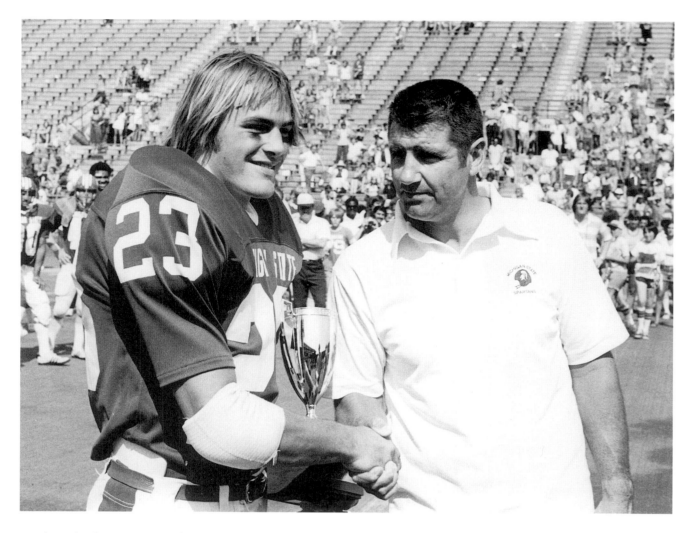

Earl Morrall, NFL quarterback and Spartan great from the '50s, passes the torch to a new generation.

And with those two advantages on my side a lot of big gains were guaranteed.

We finished our '77 season 7–3–1, 6–1–1 in the Big Ten—a half-game behind Michigan and Ohio State. And it could have been better, considering we lost 23–21 to Washington State, and tied a lowly Indiana, 13–13.

I had missed most of the Indiana game with a bruised heel, then I missed all of the next two games. It was the only time a football injury cost me any extended time. But within a few weeks my heel was better. It was getting scary at season's end, just how potent our passing game had become, and sure enough, the pro scouts were beginning to line up as we swung out of autumn '77 and into the off-season.

Early the next spring, 12 NFL teams—among them the Oakland Raiders, Dallas Cowboys, Kansas City Chiefs, and Minnesota Vikings—sent scouts to clock our best players. The event was scheduled for the indoor track at Jenison Field House.

That day I chose to be one of the last guys to run, knowing it would be to my advantage to take the time to prepare fully, and be seen. I remember warming up very methodically, very slowly, trying to establish a proper blood flow by making it easy for blood and oxygen to get to my muscles.

I walked around, shook my legs and body, getting real relaxed, trying to establish peak circulation to produce my best performance. And then I ran. And the scouts just stood there, almost blankly, staring at their watches. I wasn't satisfied at all.

"I can do a lot better than that!" I yelled.

They all kind of looked at me, and one of them said, "You did pretty good, son."

"No. I want to run again."

And I did. Two more of the most thunderous 40-yard sprints I could manage.

"What'd I run?!"

Not a word from one of those guys. I was getting irritated. Finally, I asked Darryl, and all he said was, "You did just fine, Kirk."

"Well, what'd I run?"

"You only ran a 4.2."

Turns out they all had me under 4.3 seconds, between 4.20 and 4.28. The NFL guys weren't accustomed to seeing those kinds of times. Certainly not from a guy 6-3 and 227 pounds.

A while later, Gil Brandt, the Dallas Cowboys' chief talent scout, said I'd be the 1978 Heisman Trophy frontrunner. Brandt could embellish sometimes, but it was shaping up that I could be a first-round football draft pick in 1979. Exciting stuff for a guy whose goal for so many years had been to play professional football.

Our MSU football team was my first priority. It was all because of my teammates. We had come too far together—from a 4–6–1 team faced with probation to legitimate Big Ten contenders. I enjoyed them too much. The bond between us was deep, beyond anything most people—outside of tightly knit teams—could understand. I would never have walked out on those guys. Never. Not for a million dollars. Not for five million.

As I drove back home to East Lansing to start my senior year, I marveled at how much had changed from the day my folks had dropped me off three years earlier. Michigan State was my home, and I was one of our team's leaders.

When we got on the football field, we just channeled all that closeness and spirit into intensity, and, more impressively, into the most hellacious offensive football machine I could ever have been a part of. Our 1978 team held the Big Ten record for scoring average per game, 41 points, until Penn State topped it in 1994.

We scored on one blazing touchdown pass after another that season. It wasn't just me. We had Gene Byrd, a real flyer, at the other wideout spot, and tight end Mark Brammer, who

"I TALKED WITH THE PRO SCOUTS WHO WERE THERE THAT DAY HE RAN THE 4.28 40'S. 'DARRYL,' THEY SAID, 'WE CLICKED OFF OUR WATCHES 'CAUSE WE HAD TO HAVE MISSED HIM ON THAT RUN.' NOBODY COULD BELIEVE IT. THEY JUST ASSUMED THEY HAD TO HAVE MISSED ON A TIME THAT GOOD."

—*Darryl Rogers,*
MSU Head Football Coach

1978. The Heisman Trophy Awards Dinner. One of the biggest moments for any college player.

I had come back for my senior year and to join my teammates in a quest for the Big Ten Championship. A basic tenet in sports is that only after achieving team goals can you enjoy personal accomplishment. Through hard work and determination as a team, we became Big Ten champions, and I went on to enjoy the rewards from personal achievements. It was icing on the cake.

With the Big Ten Championship in hand, I was invited to the Heisman Awards Dinner in New York. I was proud simply to be among so many great college athletes, and I was thrilled that night when I was named the country's outstanding receiver. I was presented with the award, and then gave my first speech, which amounted to scarcely more than the two words I can today remember: "Thank you." While standing on the podium, I felt as if that linebacker from Iowa who separated my shoulder was ready to drill me again.

Accepting the Outstanding Receiver award.

My first dropped pass of the year.

After I stammered through the acceptance "speech," I was walking back to my table, feeling really good about our year and my award, and then I made my only drop of the year—the trophy fell from my hands and broke!

went on to play for the Buffalo Bills, as the other primary receiver. We also had a bunch of good running backs—Steve Smith, Bruce Reeves, Mike Hans—who were as involved in the pass offense as our wideouts were.

Still, because he had an amazing ability to deliver the ball before a defender could close, Eddie Smith was the big reason we scored on so many long pass plays. He had amazing touch and timing. We would make our reads and find a hole in the coverage, then turn around just as the football was about to burn a hole through our jerseys.

Smith's bombs could break up a game fast, but running across the middle was my passion. There was more punishment there—some awful collisions—but I loved getting tough yardage that might soften up a secondary later in the game. Even on an incompletion, if I were running full-tilt and somebody hit me, the next time there was a good chance they wouldn't *want* to hit me.

Had we hung onto Smith, our triggerman, at the start of the '78 season, I'm convinced the worst we would have finished that year was 10–1. But after going up on Purdue, 14–0, early in the opener, we lost Smith when he broke his hand scoring our second TD. Our offense was paralyzed, and we ended up losing, 21–14. By the fourth game of the season, Smith was healed and we were back in our rhythm, but we missed an opportunity to beat Joe Montana and the Irish, losing 29–25. We were 1–3, and about to face nationally ranked Michigan, our arch rival—in Ann Arbor.

We shocked all the experts with a huge upset of Michigan, 24–15. It was the game that ultimately made us Big Ten co-champions—and launched us to an amazing 8–3 season. It would have sent us to the Rose Bowl had it not been our final year of probation. Then came the torchings: 49–14 over Indiana, 55–2 over Wisconsin, 59–19 at Illinois, 33–9 over Minnesota, 52–3 at Northwestern, and 42–7 over Iowa in my final football game as a Spartan.

My only regret is that I missed part of that final game, at home against the Hawkeyes. I got tossed in the second half, all because of this pistol cornerback, Mario Pace, who played as if he were under orders to get me out of the game if the Hawkeyes couldn't contain me.

First series of the game. Third play. I got a pass across the middle, against double coverage, shook the defenders, and scored a 54-yard touchdown. Over on Iowa's sideline, the decision must have been made to deploy Operation Mario.

Following the TD, every time I came off the line of scrimmage to block this guy, he would either grab me, hold me,

> "THE BIGGEST THING I REMEMBER IS THAT MINNESOTA GAME, OUR SENIOR YEAR, WHEN THEIR GUY PICKED OFF THAT FUMBLE IN THE END ZONE IN MID-AIR AND RETURNED IT DOWN THE SIDE-LINES. GIBSON WAS ON THE OTHER SIDE OF THE FIELD. I REMEMBER CHASING THE GUY—I COULDN'T COME ANYWHERE NEAR HIM. NO ONE COULD. THEN I REMEMBER GIBBY BLOWING PAST EVERYBODY AND RIPPING HIM DOWN."
>
> —*Eddie Smith,*
> *MSU quarterback in 1978*

MSU vs. Michigan—always one of our biggest games.

punch me in the stomach, or jerk my face mask. It was all very flagrant, but the officials totally ignored it, even after I hollered at them to keep an eye out. By the second half, things were out of hand, and I overreacted.

Pace rammed me in the gut, and I blew up. I picked him up by the face mask and body-slammed him to the turf. I remember kind of hunching over him after I'd flipped him, then noticing this huge lineman coming after me. I sprang on him like a tiger and threw my forearm into his chin, and right then and there I yelled a challenge to fight the whole damned Iowa team. They took me up on the offer.

I had about 20 guys on me—a hell of a donnybrook. Luckily, they got everything cleared up pretty quickly, but I was ejected from the game. There wasn't anything left to do but walk off the field and head for the bench, where I would spend the remainder of my final day as a Michigan State athlete. I had lost control over myself, and later that day, I cried—literally cried—over ending my college football career in such a humiliating way.

Ejected in my final game.

CHAPTER *five*

IT'S A QUESTION FOR WHICH I STILL DON'T HAVE A PERFECT

ANSWER. WITH EVERYTHING GOING SO SMOOTHLY IN FOOT-

BALL FOLLOWING MY JUNIOR YEAR OF COLLEGE, AND WITH A

FIRST-ROUND SLOT IN THE 1979 NFL DRAFT ALL BUT STARING ME IN

THE FACE, WHY THIS STRANGE CURIOSITY TO FOLLOW UP ON DANNY LITWHILER'S SUGGESTION TO

THINK ABOUT PLAYING BASEBALL IN THE SPRING OF MY JUNIOR YEAR?

Litwhiler was Michigan State's baseball coach and a man always in search of ways to help his program. The kind of feedback he had been getting from some of his players—guys I had played against in summer leagues—really chewed at him. They had all been telling Danny to give me a try, that I might make a difference with my speed and my power potential.

Litwhiler and I ran into each other at the Grand Rapids Football Bust, just after our '77 football season had wrapped up.

"Gibby," he said, "why don't you come out for baseball?"

As kids often do, I had always ignored my dad's previous advice, correct or not, to play baseball. I was attending Michigan State on a football scholarship. I was a football player exclusively. But I liked Danny, and maybe thinking of my dad's prodding, told Litwhiler it was worth some thought. I'm not sure it was serious until Darryl Rogers mentioned it to me shortly thereafter.

"Why not give it a try?" Rogers asked. "You've got notions of going to the NFL. If you can have decent success in baseball, it will give you some leverage for the NFL draft."

Right after the Grand Rapids Bust, Litwhiler had approached Rogers, who probably surprised Danny by endorsing the idea. But that was another thing about Darryl—he had always supported the idea of a football player participating in other sports. His philosophy was: You only get to do this college thing once. Make it as full an experience as possible, which benefits everyone.

Besides, I didn't need spring football practice, and Darryl didn't need me hanging around and possibly getting hurt.

I agreed to come out for Litwhiler's winter drills. I hadn't played baseball seriously in a couple of years. But I liked the competitiveness of it. The guys were fun, and there were moments, even while practicing indoors, when I thought there was hope of becoming a good ballplayer.

We had a batting cage set up inside the Men's Intramural Building that enabled us to take some swings prior to our spring trip south. One afternoon, we happened to have Mike Marshall as our batting practice pitcher. Marshall had been a 1974 Cy Young Award winner with the Dodgers, and pitched for a number of major league teams into the '80s.

How hitters fared off pitches in this cage, which was surrounded by mesh netting to stop the ball after it was hit, was determined by Frank Pellerin, our assistant coach. He sat at the side of the cage and hollered "hit" or "out" depending on how well you stroked the ball. Marshall had warmed up, and was ready to show the college players why *he* was the major-leaguer.

Beginning with the first swing, I was tearing the cover off the ball. The more Marshall buckled down to show me up, the harder I was hitting them. But all I heard was Pellerin barking "fly out, ground out, fly out, fly out, ground out." This got me so mad that I smashed one that nearly ripped off the top of the cage. It was hit so pure you knew it was gone in any major-league stadium in the country.

"Out!" yelled Pellerin, who liked to keep our egos in check—certainly mine—while protecting Marshall's.

"OUT?!" I screamed.

Pellerin looked at me with this poker face, as if surely it had been an out. He must have been laughing underneath, because others were laughing out loud. That ball was smoked, and since it came off a Cy Young winner, I was chalking it up as my first major-league home run, even if our coach wasn't.

A few weeks later, we left for some sunshine on an early spring trip to Texas, at what was then Pan American University. For the week I hit .450, including a tremendous home run to right-center. I was beginning to warm up to this baseball business.

Or, rather, I was until we came back north, at which point I came within an eyelash of chucking the whole experiment. I had gone 0-for-12 in our first three games, and was feeling frustrated and embarrassed. I was thinking of quitting baseball and going back across the street to football practice where I knew the system and was already successful. It was my first introduction to the adversity of baseball—and I was ready to take the easy way out.

I began to suspect that everyone—including me—had gotten carried away with the idea of Mr. Football neatly transitioning to baseball. I was totally out of my element. After another lousy game, I sat down in the opposite dugout with my head down, now seriously contemplating calling it quits. Litwhiler spotted me.

"What's the matter?"

I told him I was sick of it all, that I was tired of going through something this demeaning, and that it seemed best to end all the nonsense before it embarrassed me, and the baseball team, any further.

Danny was a good man and former major-leaguer who had seen this happen with plenty of players. Psychology was one of

"HE HIT ONE OVER THE WILLOW TREES AND OVER THE RIVER AND OVER THE ROAD AND PRACTICALLY OVER THE UNION BUILDING."

—*Dan Litwhiler,*
MSU Head Baseball Coach

his strengths. He reminded me how well I had hit in Texas, and that the pitching up north was no better. He predicted that I'd come out of a short slump as quickly as I had slipped into it.

He still wasn't sure if I was coming back—and I wasn't either. As I left the field that night and headed home, I could picture myself back on the football field at spring practice, playing the game I loved most, completely comfortable with football's routine.

But I couldn't bring myself to quit. In retrospect, one thing that helped me make the right decision was my upbringing. It was my parents' influence. I had been taught never to abandon a serious challenge, and this didn't qualify as a time to start.

Coach Litwhiler and his assistants, Pellerin and Tom Smith, constantly encouraged me to fight through the slump. I would come back to the dugout, cussing and demoralized over a strikeout, and they would say to me: "Don't get down. You've got another at-bat yet. You can hit a home run next time and win the game for us!"

They were right. The next day I hit a home run that started me on a tear. I had fought off major temptation to bag baseball, and, maybe for the first time in this sport, I began to realize

My very raw approach to hitting in my only MSU baseball season.

I BEGAN TO REALIZE MY IMPACT

COULD BE MORE IMPORTANT THAN

MY STATISTICS. MY TEAMMATES

WERE RELYING ON ME, AND I WANTED

TO BE THE GUY AT THE PLATE WITH

THE GAME ON THE LINE.

my impact could be more important than my statistics. My teammates were relying on me, and I wanted to be the guy at the plate with the game on the line.

I finished with a .390 batting average and set a couple of MSU single-season records, with 16 home runs and 52 runs batted in. In one eight-game stretch, I hit 10 home runs, including 6 in two days. Three of those homers came in the second game of a doubleheader at Northwestern, as dozens of pro scouts watched.

Pitchers couldn't throw the ball past me as we got into May, and I rocked a couple of pitches that are still talked about. A few cleared trees that bordered East Lansing's Red Cedar River. I hit another ball during batting practice at the University of Michigan that sailed beyond the roof of the Track and Tennis Building, which was roughly equivalent to clearing the roof at Tiger Stadium. All this might explain why, at the end of the season, my aluminum bat was flat on one side.

The scouts, though, love speed as much as power. My ability to steal bases—21 in 22 tries—was another reason major-league clubs were studying me so closely and talking me up to the national press.

The season had taught me a great lesson in life, which I would later have to relearn. I had come within an eyelash of leaving a team, and four weeks later I was on my way to being named first team All-American, in step with the first team All-American status I would receive that fall in football. I not only seemed headed for the first round of the 1979 NFL draft, but now I also had major-league clubs saying I might be the first baseball player selected in the June draft of 1978.

I began to hear from people like Jim Martz of the Major League Scouting Bureau, one of baseball's best bird dogs, who said I was a top prospect. Paul Snyder, who was minor-league administrator for the Atlanta Braves, later said I had the best combination of speed and power he had seen. That statement was the start of some of those Mickey Mantle comparisons.

Snyder's quote on the 1978 draft crop appeared everywhere: "Gibson stands out. The rest are a box entry." Atlanta wanted to select me with the draft's first pick, and the Seattle Mariners were hoping to grab me at the sixth spot. The New York Yankees owner, George Steinbrenner, had also shown a big interest.

Another club in pursuit was the Detroit Tigers, a team I had spent my entire life following, even adoring. The Tigers had been keeping an eye on me since the time of our March trip to Texas. Bill Lajoie, the club's assistant general manager and top scout, had gotten a dazzling report on me and passed on instructions to the rest of the Tigers scouting staff: Do not scout Gibson in

East Lansing—check him out only on the road. The Tigers were trying to conceal their interest in hopes of keeping other clubs cool to me. But by mid-May, I was no longer anyone's secret.

As the baseball draft talk continued, I remained firm on my commitment to my college football teammates: I was coming back to play at MSU in the fall. I would not forfeit my senior year of eligibility. I didn't care what team, offering whatever amount of money, drafted me. Unless it could be arranged so that I could play football as a senior, I wasn't signing.

I learned soon after all the first-round noise began that I could, under NCAA rules, play professional baseball and still finish my eligibility in football. It enabled me to throw a shell game at clubs that were selecting ahead of the one team I wanted to sign with—the Detroit Tigers, if they wanted me.

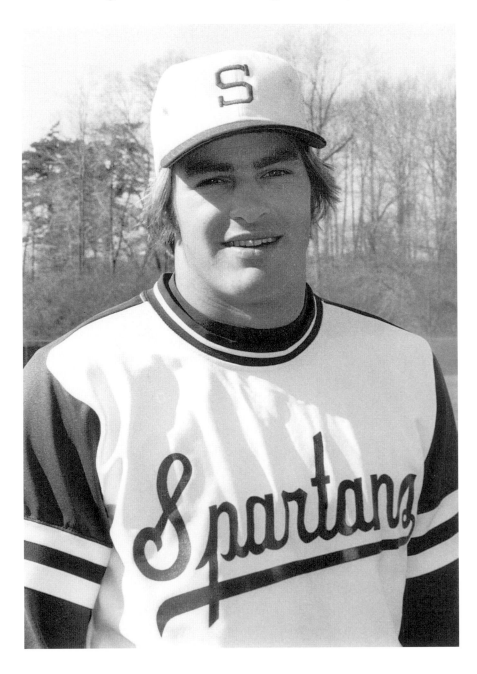

"HE SAID, 'MR. DIDIER, I WANT YOU TO KNOW I PROMISED COACH ROGERS THAT NO MATTER WHAT HAPPENED WITH BASEBALL, I DEFINITELY WOULD GO BACK AND FINISH MY SENIOR YEAR OF ELIGIBILITY. YOU COULD OFFER ME A MILLION DOLLARS RIGHT NOW, AND I'M NOT GOING BACK ON MY WORD.' I'LL TELL YOU WHAT, BROTHER, THIS GUY IS FOR REAL WHEN HE TELLS YOU THAT."

—Mel Didier,
Seattle Mariner's Scout (1978)

With no advance notice, the Tigers called and quickly and discreetly arranged to bring me to Tiger Stadium for a round of pre-game batting practice. It was two weeks before the baseball draft. They wanted to see me perform on the field, surrounded by the same players and the same atmosphere I would be dealing with on the major-league level.

I drove down on Saturday morning, getting more and more excited the closer I got to the corner of Michigan and Trumbull, the famous intersection at Tiger Stadium. I had been going to this stadium since I was a kid, and I was pumped that I might be playing for the Tigers, in my hometown, in front of my friends and family. I had sat in those then-green seats, cheering for Al Kaline and Norm Cash and Mickey Lolich. I had pounded a bat on the concrete floor, the way 25,000 other kids always did on Bat Day, which was a longtime promotion always held conveniently near my birthday.

I walked down the stadium concourse and was taken into an auxiliary room where I could change into my uniform and spikes. It was nearly three hours before game time, but the key people—Tiger manager Ralph Houk and his coaches—were already on the field waiting for me to dress and grab a bat. They wanted to watch me take batting practice and then get me out of there fast before the rest of the world knew what was cooking.

I walked down the dark tunnel that leads into the Tiger dugout. Dick Tracewski, who was one of Houk's coaches, was on the mound waiting to pitch to me. I grabbed the first bat that looked good—the biggest, heaviest bat in the rack—which belonged to their rugged catcher Lance Parrish. My first adjustment to the big leagues hit me right there. Wood. I hadn't swung a wooden bat in over two years.

I stepped into the batter's box—every kid's dream—and took in a scene that was absolutely electric: Emerald-green grass. Players dressed in Detroit's classic white and blue uniforms, and this great, double-decked—triple-decked in right field—stadium that from home plate stood like a castle surrounding a courtyard.

Beginning with his first pitch, I hammered everything. I don't know how many pitches crashed into the upper deck, but during a lengthy, 60-pitch session, it was more than enough to have sold the Tigers on my raw ability.

Houk had managed the Yankees during their '60s heyday, and he knew a lot about raw talent. But it was seeing how the other players responded that confirmed it was not a normal batting practice. Word had spread as I continued ripping Tracewski's pitches: "Check this guy out." Players stopped their normal routine to see for themselves.

I was actually getting static from a few of the players, which was *their* test to see if I belonged. "Throw him a curveball, Trixie," Lance Parrish yelled, using Tracewski's nickname. "See if he can hit that out."

Naturally, with my football demeanor, I was instantly seething. I stared at Parrish, giving him one of those "mind your own business" looks, and I recall muttering that he ought to shut his mouth as I continued hammering the ball. Later I would come to know Lance Parrish as one of life's great people.

I dressed and left the ballpark. No one said much to me—almost like my early freshman days at Michigan State—but everyone knew what had happened. It was an awesome experience—but I couldn't share it with anyone because the Tigers didn't want anyone to find out the results of this "secret" tryout.

I talked with Lajoie the next day, and he asked me to give him a rough figure on what it would take to sign me. I had talked with my dad and with MSU assistant coach Tom Smith, a very decent man who had been in the Braves organization. We had a dollar amount in mind that we felt would be fair to both sides.

The Tigers were back in touch by the first of the week. I was going to be Detroit's first-round selection. They had the 12th pick in the first round, so I had to discourage 11 other clubs from drafting me ahead of Detroit. All I could do was use the football smokescreen and hope none of the top 11 was in a gambling mood on draft day. I was at least doing my part. I heard from nearly 15 clubs during the month preceding the draft, with every phone conversation going the same way:

"Kirk, we are very interested in making you our top draft choice. Can you tell us about your football plans?"

"I am going back and playing football for Michigan State in the fall."

"So, what you're telling us is, no matter what we offer..."

"No, what I'm telling you is that I'm coming back and playing my senior year of football."

Outside of the Tigers, clubs couldn't be sure what I was thinking. Even if they figured I might choose baseball over pro football as a career, they weren't wild about exposing me to a senior season of football. Baseball people were also wary of what the NFL insiders were saying. Bucko Kilroy, a scout for the New England Patriots, told *Sports Illustrated* I was "the first legitimate 4.2, 40-yard white man" they had ever timed. A Seattle Seahawks scout also told *SI* that on a scale of 1 to 8, I was a 9.

Either way, my resolve to play football as a senior, coupled with those first-round projections in the 1979 NFL draft, made me risky for baseball teams that could hardly afford to gamble on not signing a first-round draft pick. Only the Tigers knew for sure.

Surprisingly, George Steinbrenner's Yankees were still pushing me. Hard. He ended up sending his man Birdie Tebbetts to East Lansing for some one-on-one salesmanship. I had told Tebbetts over the phone to forget it, although I really didn't tell him why New York didn't have a chance with me.

I flat-out didn't like the Yankees. I didn't like their free-agent flesh-buying. I didn't like the way they tended to let minor-league talent, at least in my mind, languish.

Tebbetts, though, worked for Steinbrenner, who was intent on getting me.

"I've got to come out there," Tebbetts said over the phone, even after I had told him repeatedly to forget about me. "I'd like to have dinner with you and your mom and dad."

He met us at the Pretzel Bell restaurant in East Lansing, and we weren't even into our salads before Tebbetts began the pitch.

"What's it going to take to make you a part of the New York Yankees?"

Over the next 20 minutes I told him as many ways as I could that it would never happen.

Birdie, under pressure from Steinbrenner, finally said, "Look, I want to tell you something. I was sent out here and instructed not to come home until you agreed to sign with the Yankees."

I wasn't backing off.

"Birdie, you're going to have to go home without me," I said, "'cause I ain't doin' it. I will not, *under any circumstances,* agree to sign a contract with the New York Yankees."

Those who knew me had every reason to be surprised that I would agree to play professional baseball over football. Football was the game I loved most. I was built for football. I was 6'3", 227 pounds, and I was mean. Football was easier for me. Baseball was mental. Football, you took your failures and frustrations out on someone else—physically. You caught the ball. You ran with it. You hit people. You played with all-out intensity. Everything about football played to my strengths.

Baseball, conversely, was unbelievably difficult. Especially hitting, where a batter's challenge is to hit a 90-mph baseball that's moving in all sorts of evil ways.

At football I could always expect to excel. In baseball, I could look forward to a regular date with humility. And there were no guarantees that I would even make it. But this was a long-term decision. Baseball was hot. It had free agency. Its players had longer careers, which would give me a better opportunity to win a championship. I even looked over the Basic Player Agreements in the NFL and in Major League Baseball, and there was no comparison as to which sport took better long-term care of its players. Even though football was my emotional choice, objectively I had to choose baseball—and, in the process, prepare myself for plenty of embarrassment and frustration.

The Tigers had a pretty good idea how each of the clubs ahead of them would select in the '78 draft, and they were worried mainly about one team: Seattle, whose chief scouts, Mel Didier and Jerry Krause, really liked me.

The Mariners were pushing hard. Krause, a great multi-sport scout who is now the Chicago Bulls general manager, met me, accompanied by Smith, for dinner at the Holiday Inn in Howell, Michigan. The Mariners saw me as the big building-block in a franchise that at the time was only a year old.

Krause and Didier had gone nuts after watching my home run barrage at Northwestern. "He reminds me of Mickey Mantle, with Pete Rose hustle," Didier had written on his scouting report. "He has a flair."

Krause, likewise, thought I was precisely what the Mariners needed. He gave me a sales pitch on Seattle that the Chamber of Commerce could not have matched. And he and Didier had no problem allowing me to return to East Lansing for my senior year of football.

It was all set up. They called Seattle's front-office boss, Lou Gorman, and told him Seattle had its franchise player. They also mentioned the kind of money it would take to sign me, which was in the $250,000 range.

Seattle's owners—they included Danny Kaye, the entertainer—quashed the deal. They never knew of my deal with Detroit. Didier and Krause were heartsick, but the decision gave me a shot at signing with the one club I wanted to join—the Detroit Tigers.

Draft Day was agonizing as the first round dragged on, minute by minute. The Mariners ended up taking a guy named Tito Nanni, who never played in the majors. Finally, the phone rang—I'm still not sure who made the call—and a voice said: "Congratulations. You've just been drafted by the Detroit Tigers." Within a few days, I signed a $200,000 deal that would bind me to the Tigers for six years, with no renegotiation possible until I made the major leagues. I was now a week from reporting to the Lakeland Tigers, Detroit's Single A stop. It was a notch above rookie ball, which was reasonable. College, plus my raw ability, had counted for something, especially when a player like Bob Horner—whom Atlanta selected first—went straight to the majors from college.

I was to fly to Miami to meet the Lakeland team on the road and to get acquainted with my manager, Jim Leyland, a young guy who already was regarded as a Tigers manager of the future.

He met me at the gate and we shook hands.

> **"I HAD THE SAME FEELING SEEING GIBSON THAT I HAD WHEN I FIRST SAW EARL MONROE IN A MIDNIGHT NAIA GAME IN KANSAS CITY BACK IN THE '60S. THE ONLY OTHER TIME I HAD THAT FEELING WAS WHEN I FIRST SAW SCOTTIE PIPPEN. GIBSON WAS THE SINGLE BEST PROSPECT I HAD SEEN IN 16 YEARS OF SCOUTING."**
>
> *—Jerry Krause,*
> *Chicago Bulls general manager,*
> *ex-scout*

Waiting for the call in my college apartment.

"Hi, Kirk. Jim Leyland."

He was polite, but very business-like. We small-talked our way to the luggage conveyor, picked up my bags, and as we drove off the airport service road Leyland rolled up the windows and tore into me like a German Shepherd. "Kirk Gibson, I don't care how much money you're making! I don't care how big of a bonus baby you are! I don't give a damn what you did in football, or what you did playing college baseball!

"I'm the manager down here, and you will do what I say. Every day! You carry no weight with me or with this team, and you will not expect any special or preferential treatment. And if you don't like it, that's tough, because I am here to stay, and you do not at this point in your career know one damn thing about playing this game. All you have is raw ability, and it's my job to make sure you develop that ability. Is that understood?

"Now, here's what's going to happen: You will be at the stadium every morning at 8:30 a.m. And I will be there with you. And we will throw. And we will catch. And we will work on all imaginable fundamentals. Then, you can go home and get lunch, and come back and work out with the rest of the team. *Then* you can play a game."

It jolted me but didn't intimidate me. I could understand what he was saying even then. He was the boss. I was a rookie with everything to learn about baseball, and I could forget about anything that had preceded today.

After this scorching, I looked him directly in the eye, and just said: "Fine. Fine with me."

We got started that week on the retooling of a rookie, and it was serious labor. Two hours, minimum, each morning under a roasting Florida sun. Leyland would throw 60 minutes of batting

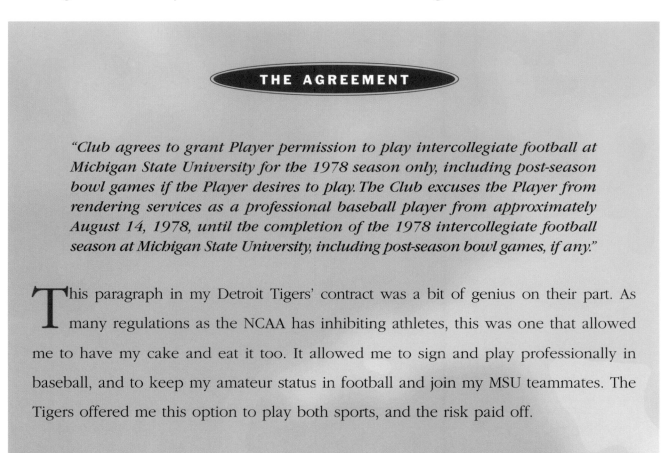

THE AGREEMENT

"Club agrees to grant Player permission to play intercollegiate football at Michigan State University for the 1978 season only, including post-season bowl games if the Player desires to play. The Club excuses the Player from rendering services as a professional baseball player from approximately August 14, 1978, until the completion of the 1978 intercollegiate football season at Michigan State University, including post-season bowl games, if any."

This paragraph in my Detroit Tigers' contract was a bit of genius on their part. As many regulations as the NCAA has inhibiting athletes, this was one that allowed me to have my cake and eat it too. It allowed me to sign and play professionally in baseball, and to keep my amateur status in football and join my MSU teammates. The Tigers offered me this option to play both sports, and the risk paid off.

Signing my first major league contract with (from left to right) Dad, Mom, Jim Campbell and Bill Lajoie.

practice or feed the pitching machine to me, and then we would adjourn to the outfield for some earnest work on defense, throwing, catching—all phases of my very amateurish game.

Leyland and I got along terrifically from the first workout. He was younger than the average manager, and very competitive, and I was coming out of college ball in great shape, physically fine-tuned. Drills became a competition between us. It helped me build strength and intensity during all those blistering days, during those endless repetitions as Leyland tried to pound some professionalism into my game. In the process we became good friends. My respect for Jim Leyland was, and still is, enormous.

I had been tossed into the lineup that first night in Miami against the Orioles' Class A club. I didn't feel particularly good about the way I played, but I wasn't down. I was more awed at the level of players I saw at Single A. It was a whole new level of play—faster pitches, better curveballs, faster double plays. The entire game was faster and more intense.

What hit me hardest was that I would have to adjust to this new level of intensity immediately. Not only were we playing a baseball game every night, but morning and afternoon work-outs turned each day into a 15-hour doubleheader.

On top of that, there was the travel. Long bus trips through the South. Meals at Pizza Hut or out of a Burger King bag. Cheap food and cheap hotels were the norm.

Home for me was the Holiday Inn Central in Lakeland, Florida. Rooms were at least air-conditioned, so after lunch, about the only thing to do was to stretch out across the bed, watch a little TV, and try and rest up from the morning work-out. By 3:30 it would be time to head back to our home field, Marchant Stadium, where the Detroit Tigers were always based during spring training.

I was only in Florida for eight weeks before returning to Michigan State, which was part of my agreement with the Tigers. My numbers had been unimpressive: Fifty-four games. A .240 batting average in 175 at-bats, with eight home runs, and 40 runs knocked in. Seventeen of my 42 hits were for extra bases. I had 13 stolen bases, made six errors, and struck out 54 times.

Leyland, though, had been on my side from day one, handling me perfectly. He knew when to pat me on the back—which wasn't a lot at that point—and he knew how to stay on my butt. And not only with me, but with everybody. He demanded that you play the game of baseball right.

It had been a challenging summer. We won enough games the second half of the season to put us in the playoffs, but I had to go back to Michigan State for two-a-day practices to prepare for my final football season. After winning the Big Ten Championship, my football days were finished, and I went back to focusing on my commitment to baseball.

> **"I NEVER, EVER HAD ANYONE WHO WORKED HARDER THAN HIM. NEVER. EVER. WITHOUT QUESTION, HE IS THE MOST FIERCE COMPETITOR I'VE EVER MANAGED IN MY LIFE."**
>
> —*Jim Leyland,*
> *Florida Marlins manager who*
> *managed Gibson in the minor leagues*
> *and in Pittsburgh*

Lakeland Tigers, 1978.

The next spring I was juiced about heading to Lakeland, Florida, for my first spring training with the Tigers. No one truly expected me to make the team, but that group didn't include me.

The Tigers were building. Why would I not fit into the picture? I wanted to show the front office, and this new manager, Les Moss, that I belonged on the team and could help them win. This was the level of play I wanted to be at, and I would raise my level in order to be there.

Early workouts were promising. I was still raw, but I hit the ball hard in batting practice and during intra-squad games, and, as always, my aggressive running attracted attention.

We played Boston in our first Grapefruit League game, at Lakeland. I was batting in the eighth inning against a right-hander named Win Remmerswaal when he threw me a sweet 3–1 fastball that I knocked over the right center field fence, a good 425 feet. It was my first home run in a Tiger uniform and I wanted to dispel any notions the Tigers had of ticketing me to Triple A ball, as I was focused on making the major-league team.

Another bit of excitement and publicity was generated with the proposed race between myself and Ron LeFlore, who was the fastest man to have worn a Tigers uniform during the '70s. It was all the result of some locker-room joshing.

LeFlore loved to kid, and figured a rookie with a reputation for being a sprinter was irresistible. We went back and forth, giving each other a lot of loud grief, and before long The Race was on.

LeFlore vs. Gibson. Forty yards. And for a fair amount of money. We were talking various wagers, I remember, in the thousands of dollars, which led LeFlore to say: "Let's get somebody to put the money up, and we'll split it 50-50." I barked back, "Fifty-fifty! You're dreaming. Winner take all."

The Detroit media picked up on it, and our match race was shaping up as one of the better stories during a sleepy stage of spring.

Jim Campbell, the Tigers' president, found out about it, and we were quietly told by him, "We're not here to race, we're here to win baseball games. Let's get our priorities in order."

After the race was called off, I continued to focus on making the first round of cuts. I was playing well, leading the team in home runs early on, and ready in my mind to make the squad and head north. Les Moss was the new Tigers manager, and he had been pretty much noncommittal about me when the press quizzed him. That all changed when the first round of cuts was made. Moss called me into his office and said I was being assigned to the Triple A team that would be heading back to Evansville in a couple of weeks.

I was devastated—and furious. I saw no reason why, after my start, I didn't even make the first cut on a team that plainly needed help and wouldn't be hurt with me "learning" to play at that top level.

Getting past the early snub was difficult, and I didn't feel any better the next day when the first of my baseball injuries arrived in my first Triple A exhibition game. I hurt my knee in a collision in the outfield diving for a ball, and was out for a month. It was a serious emotional drop after being on such a high.

I had arthroscopic surgery on the knee, and they found there was no serious ligament damage. It was a bad contusion—a significant bruise. It would be a month before I would report to Triple A Evansville and to the new manager there, Jim Leyland, who had been promoted from Lakeland. Leyland and I resumed our grueling morning workouts in Evansville, where it seemed even hotter than it had been in Florida.

At least I could look forward to a season with Leyland. Getting better under his watch would take some of the sting out of playing minor league baseball in a hot, humid, Ohio River town that, for all its Midwest character, was a long way from the major-league cities I thought I should be seeing.

I went through another lesson-every-day campaign: .245 average in 89 games, 9 home runs, 42 runs batted in, and 20 stolen bases. Plus, I finished hot, helping us to win our division and take the league title in the playoffs.

On September 5, 1979, Leyland called me in my hotel room in Springfield, Illinois, the morning after we had won the league championship.

"They want you in Detroit," he said. "Get on up there. Congratulations."

Sports Illustrated

MARCH 24, 1980 $1.25

RIP-ROARIN' ROOKIE

**Detroit Centerfielder
Kirk Gibson**

NCAA BASKETBALL

CHAPTER *six*

I SAT IN THE DUGOUT WONDERING WHEN SPARKY ANDERSON WOULD GIVE UP AND PUT A FIDGETING ROOKIE INTO THE GAME. IT WAS GETTING INTO THE LATE INNINGS AGAINST THE NEW YORK YANKEES, AND I WAS NOT MUCH INTO THE CONCEPT OF BEING A HUMBLE, OBEDIENT BENCHWARMER. THREE DAYS HAD PASSED SINCE MY CALL-UP TO THE TIGERS ON SEPTEMBER 5, 1979.

I wanted to play. Even if big, menacing Goose Gossage and his 100-mph fastball had shown up for a ninth-inning closer at Tiger Stadium, I wanted out of the dugout and onto the field.

There were probably better guys to take your first major-league at-bat against. Gossage was awesome—the best and most monstrous relief pitcher in the game. He wore a Fu Manchu mustache and threw a baseball at such blinding speed that you'd be lucky to see it, let alone hit it.

Big deal. I was so revved to play that in the late innings I began to parade and strut in our dugout. I was pacing around, making sure that I was all but in the face of Sparky Anderson, Detroit's new manager, who had not yet been on the job 90 days. Managers and coaches were always looking for the same thing: They wanted gamers. And I wanted a shot at Gossage.

I went over to the bat rack and began picking up bats and feeling them out.

"What the hell are you doing?" asked Anderson, who was half-amused that I wanted into a game against this guy.

"I want him," I said.

"You want him," Sparky answered, "get your bat."

There were two outs and we were down by a run when he sent me into my first major-league game as a pinch-hitter.

I hopped from the dugout with a bat in my hands and went to the on-deck circle for a couple of twirls and some hard swings that I barely felt. Since I was supposed to be Detroit's new superstar, the crowd stood up to see what the press had been talking about. My body was half-numb with energy. Just because I ached to play did not mean this 21-year-old rookie was in command of his emotions.

I was about ready to explode from the rushing adrenaline as the public-address speakers boomed my name and the crowd roared even louder, and the big roof-mounted light towers burned with the intensity of spotlights.

Gossage didn't waste any time. He cranked up and threw a blistering fastball that I must have begun swinging at before it left his fingertips. I had a good cut at the ball and fouled it straight back against the screen. You could hear the crowd "ooohhhhh" as I swung.

Gossage went through the same routine against everyone, whether he was a rookie or an

My first spring training for the Tigers.

All-Star. He didn't fool around with signs. He just looked in at the catcher, nodded with a jerk of his head, wound up, and said, "Here it is, kid, come get it." More heat was on its way.

I fouled his second heater against the screen. The crowd again went "ooohhhhh" in unison. I could not believe how hard this guy threw. He just shook his head again, sort of like a bull ready to charge, then wound up and threw another blazer that was hissing as it blew past me.

Steeerrrike three! You could smell the heat from the friction as his fastball tore into the catcher's mitt. The crowd moaned in disappointment, but judging from the stadium buzz that followed, it was clear everyone enjoyed the confrontation.

If there was any consolation, it was knowing at-bats couldn't get any tougher than this in the big leagues. No one threw like Gossage, and no one could have abused me more in my Detroit Tigers baptism.

Afterward I found myself feeling angry and disappointed that I let down the fans, who were looking for something dramatic. In reality, though, a guy like Gossage could virtually own you, making a bat seem like pretty slim artillery against a 100-mph baseball.

A couple of weeks later we were in Baltimore, with Steve Stone pitching for the Orioles, when I hit my first big-league home run. It was a drive into the right center field bleachers at old Memorial Stadium, and it came on one of those junk-ball change-ups that Stone typically threw. I managed to get the ball back, streaked with green paint from where it crashed into the seats.

I finished my four-week Tigers cameo with enough of a package—a .237 average, 1 home run, 4 RBIs, and 3 stolen bases—to win over Sparky, even if he figured it would be a thousand big-league at-bats before I really knew what I was doing at the plate. When Detroit began planning for 1980, Sparky had made up his mind on what to do with Kirk Gibson.

"I know everybody feels he should start at Triple A," Sparky said to Jim Campbell, Detroit's general manager. "But if he does—and I may be mistaken on this—I believe if you put him at Triple A, he's going to play on that level only.

"On the other hand, if you force him to play at his best level, I think we have a different horse here. I think we have one here who needs to be challenged."

"Then that," Campbell said, "is what we'll do."

There were careful plans emerging as part of the club's blueprint for building an '80s contender. They centered around some developing starting pitchers, such as Jack Morris, and four up-the-middle talents: Lance Parrish behind the plate, Alan Trammell and Lou Whitaker in the infield, and me in center, which is where I was headed after Detroit traded Ron LeFlore to Montreal for a left-handed pitcher, Dan Schatzeder.

Anderson had seen enough of these players to understand that he had thoroughbreds on his hands. He wanted to be sure the brashness I exhibited was part of my warrior's profile, that it was calculated rather than reckless.

Sparky decided to get some answers when he invited me to his home in Thousand Oaks, California, for a few days during the winter. We worked out at a nearby small college and talked

NO ONE THREW LIKE GOSSAGE, AND NO ONE COULD HAVE ABUSED ME MORE IN MY DETROIT TIGERS BAPTISM.

Over-aggressiveness throughout my career involved me in some unusual plays. Tops on the list was an incident against Boston in 1983 when I KO'd home plate umpire Larry Barnett. Lou Whitaker was on second with one out when I hit a towering drive to deep center (440 ft.). I headed around first at full speed and by the time the ball careened off the screen, and back onto the field, I was only 20 feet behind Whitaker at second. He had been holding up, waiting to see if the ball would be caught. Third base coach Alex Grammas waved Whitaker home, and I was so close to Whitaker that I thought the signal was intended for me. Barnett, who had stepped across the foul line to make the call on Whitaker at home—the relay was in time to nail Lou—stepped directly into my path, and I smoked him. Barnett went flying, with all of the extra baseballs exploding from his pouch, as I tagged home plate.

Whitaker was called out, Barnett was knocked out, and first base umpire Ken Kaiser called me safe, pointing to one of the five base-balls that was on the ground. It caused quite an argument-until everyone noticed that Barnett wasn't moving. Medical personnel took him off the field on a stretcher,

One of the strangest plays in my career.

although he wasn't seriously hurt and was back on the job the following day. That's when I presented him with a football helmet with a Detroit "D" on it, and offered a bit of advice that he put it on the next time he set up for a play at the plate.

What made that game even crazier is that I hit a home run all the way out of Tiger Stadium, onto the roof of a lumber company, a blast that measured 523 feet.

Learning from one of baseball's greats, Sparky Anderson.

baseball nonstop back at his house. Sparky came to like two things about me: the level of smarts I displayed, and the fact that I was courteous to his family and to others—which seemed like pretty basic stuff from my corner.

Sparky, a keen manager who picked up on important details, had noticed something else that was new to him. He saw for the first time the ways football influenced a baseball prospect. There was, in his mind, a coachability and a mental toughness that could only have been shaped in football, a performance-oriented thing that stood separate from personal traits.

I was not going back to Triple A because Anderson was committed to playing me in Detroit. I did nothing in spring training to lose my job as Detroit's new center fielder, but I also did little to show that this would be a smooth transition, not with the way I could get fooled at the plate, or more glaringly, get turned around in the field. In promoting me so early, the Tigers had bought an up-and-down ride in an effort to put my game on the top end of the learning curve.

In 1980 *Sports Illustrated* put me on the cover of its spring training issue, bumping up the Mickey Mantle index a few

Jack Billingham was a 6-foot-5 right-hander who had pitched for Sparky in Cincinnati before joining the Tigers in 1978. He believed that kids fresh from the minors, as I was in 1980, deserved to be treated one way and one way only—disrespectfully—which was not a philosophy I shared.

With Billingham it was always, "Rookie this, rookie that...rookie, rookie, rookie." To my way of thinking, it was no different than when I had broken in at Michigan State, believing that veteran players or All-State recruits merited no more respect from me than I deserved from them.

"This rookie stuff don't cut it with me," I had told Billingham, and added, with a gesture, "So, you can rookie this." A few hours before a game early in the season, I walked through the swinging doors that led toward the training room and Billingham was at it again.

"Oh, boy, there goes the rook back into the training room," he started in on me, "what kind of wonderful treatment are we getting today, rook?"

He barged through the doors and in a split second I decided I had taken my last razzing, ever, from this guy.

I exploded at him with my forearm leading, and Billingham, all 230 pounds of him, went flying back through the swinging doors, and was falling to the floor as I jumped on top of him.

"ROOKIE ME ONE MORE TIME!" I screamed. "YOU SAY ONE MORE WORD, AND I'LL RIP YOUR WINDPIPE RIGHT OUT OF YOUR THROAT! YOU'LL NEVER TALK AGAIN! YOU HEAR ME?!"

The guys in the clubhouse were frozen.

"Hey, man, I was just screwing around," Billingham wailed. He was still stretched out on the floor, and, as out of my mind as I appeared, he couldn't quite be sure I wasn't going to kill him right there on the spot.

"I'M THROUGH WITH YOU SCREWING WITH ME," I yelled back. Then I challenged the rest of the guys, who were standing like statues in front of their lockers.

"THE HELL WITH ALL YOU GUYS!" I shouted, looking across the room. "ANYBODY ELSE WANT ME? C'MON, LET'S GO! WE'LL PUT THIS ROOKIE THING TO REST RIGHT NOW!" Stone cold silence.

Then I nodded and said, calmly but firmly: "Thank you."

Actually, Billingham and I got along fine—afterward. But to me the whole rookie initiation rite was stupid, and alien to the purpose for which a team played.

*The incredible force of
swinging a bat.*

notches as we opened our 1980 season in Kansas City. The Royals were starting their red-bearded, high-kicking right-hander, Dennis Leonard, and I could expect to see lots of high heat. I knocked one of his upstairs fastballs into the second water fountain in right center field for a home run. I also belted a triple, as we won, 5–1, marking a new trend in a stadium that through the years had been poison for Detroit.

Back in Detroit for Opening Day, I badly misplayed a fly ball, reminding everyone of the rawness of my game. I was learning hard lessons in one of the most public and high-profile classrooms in America, but I was also producing fairly well, and I was learning to play at this new level. I was able to justify the faith Sparky Anderson had had in me when he lobbied to keep me in Detroit.

Eight weeks into the season I was progressing at a pace the Tigers and I could view as promising. I was leading the team in home runs, batting .260 to .270, striking out about once every four at-bats, and holding my own in center field.

We went into Milwaukee for a series during the first weekend of June, and in the Saturday night game I hit an early home run off Buster Keeton, which was my ninth of the season. He threw me a change-up during my next at-bat, and after first committing, I tried to check my swing and felt a pop in my wrist as I was trying to hold up.

I didn't think a lot about it afterward—not until I awakened the next morning in my room at the Pfister Hotel. Then I got scared. I could not move my left hand. Radiating from my wrist was a terrible pain.

For weeks I couldn't play as the injury totally baffled doctors. My wrist was placed in a cast to rest it. After a few weeks there was still no improvement. Finally, the Tigers, my doctors, and I agreed the only thing to do was visit the Mayo Clinic in Rochester, Minnesota, for a second opinion.

It was August before I got the diagnosis from Dr. James Dobyns. I had a freakish injury produced by an abnormal physical development. The ulna bone in my arm, which is supposed to be the same length or shorter than the radius bone, wasn't. Under the kind of stress produced by swinging a baseball bat, the ulna had pinched and shredded my triangular fibro cartilage.

The doctors proposed shortening the ulna and inserting a steel plate to stabilize the area. Surgery was ordered for August 22, followed by eight to nine months of rehabilitation. Not only was my rookie season finished, but there was no guarantee I would return in 1981. Not one doctor gave me any assurance that I would ever play baseball again.

The doctors had to cut down the ulna, then insert a steel plate to stabilize the area. The steel plate would stay in my wrist for nearly two years. And I expected them to guarantee that I would productively swing a baseball bat at a 100-mph fastball?

I don't know who was more devastated—me, or the Tigers—at the thought that I might be finished after having played four months, total, of big-league baseball. It was an emotional and psychological blindside, and one thought kept cropping up over and over: I had risked throwing away a big NFL career to have all of this happen, when longevity was one of the major reasons I had chosen baseball.

The only news that gave me any hope was that the doctors speculated the injury would not prevent me from playing football. Swinging a baseball bat was one thing. Catching a football, running, and blocking was another. It didn't put the same pinpointed stress on my wrist. Even in the NFL.

The St. Louis Cardinals had drafted me in the seventh round, reasoning that if things didn't work out in baseball, or if I got hurt, they would have merely invested a late-round pick on a shot at a game-breaker. Though it hadn't mattered before, I was

I always took pride in being a leader.

optimistic about it now, especially since the doctors were so guarded about my recovery.

But the football option never had to develop, as I followed my rehab plan perfectly and got back to the Tigers by the following spring. No one could be absolutely sure as we arrived in Lakeland that the wrist would hold up. I tested it gradually, and waited until later into spring training before I actually gave the wrist its first full-throttle test against live pitching.

I made it through Florida with no setbacks, and convinced the doctors that my surgery had done the job. We were to open the 1981 regular season in Detroit, against Toronto, and I expected to be starting in center field, where I had been working throughout spring training.

I got to Tiger Stadium on Opening Day, all juiced and ready to go after almost a year off from baseball. I walked into the clubhouse and checked the lineup card that was always taped on the wall outside Sparky Anderson's office. There was a "9" next to my name. I was starting in right field, which made no sense. I stepped in to see the boss.

"Hey, Sparky, I think you made a mistake on the lineup. There's a 9 beside my name."

He was sitting in there, smoking his pipe, signing a box of baseballs. He never looked up.

"Oh, no," he said. "There's no mistake."

"But I haven't played right field the entire spring."

"Go get 'em, kid," Sparky said, his eyes lighting up. "I know you can do it."

I had never played right field at Tiger Stadium. Never. And at this ballpark moving to right was no simple shift from center field. The angle of the sun in right field at Tiger Stadium means you look almost straight into blinding light on any high fly ball hit during mid-day. Then there's the matter of the right field upper deck, which in Detroit actually hangs over the warning track. A deep fly ball can disappear as you wait for it, then

Fighting the sun.

"YOU SHOW ME WHEN HE'S NOT GIVING 100 PERCENT AND I'LL BOO HIM, TOO."

—*Barbara Gibson*

reappear a few feet above your head, all depending on how high and how deep the ball is hit.

As I took the field for pregame warm-ups I could tell I was in trouble. The sky was deep blue, cloudless—a ceiling of glare. I had no sense of depth perception, plus I hadn't even learned how to use sunglasses with any dexterity.

Sure enough, first inning, Willie Upshaw hit a high fly ball and the sun was right square in my face. I had an angle on it for a second, and stood staring into the sun waiting for the ball, when it hit against my ear and the side of my head. It fell to the ground, and the Opening Day crowd turned on me instantly.

I missed another fly ball later in the game, one of those peekaboo specials that disappeared, then reappeared, out of the overhang. It landed next to me on the track and this time the crowd responded with an even louder chorus of boos.

Humbling—every bit of it—on a day that I was supposed to be celebrating my full-time return to a Tiger uniform. But credit Sparky with this: He had me back in the lineup the next day, starting in right field, with Ricky Peters again in center. No giving up on Gibson as a project, no matter how ugly I might look along the way.

Unfortunately, I reinjured my wrist in early May in a baserunning tumble and didn't return to the lineup for almost two months, which was the day major-league baseball restarted following a 50-day midseason strike. After the strike I hit .375—.366 against left-handers—and got at least one hit in 41 of our final 48 games. I finished the year batting .328, but didn't have enough at-bats to qualify for the batting title. Carney Lansford won it with a .336 average. More important, team-wise we had developed into a contender, and we had a chance to make the playoffs by sweeping Milwaukee in our final series. After winning the first game, we lost the second to end our bid. A key moment that day was when Sparky gave orders for every player to stay in the dugout and watch the Brewers celebrate their victory and their Division Championship. Later, in the locker room, he said, "Did everybody see that? That's what you're after. Now think about that in the off-season."

Taking time to sign autographs.

During that season I had my first dramatic high profile game-winning home run as a Tiger, a three-run rocket off Ron Davis of the Yankees during a Sunday afternoon game in mid-August at Tiger Stadium. The Yankees were leading, 4–2, with two runners on base and two out in the ninth. Davis cut loose with a fastball and I ripped the mother through a big wind into the upper-deck bleachers in deep right center field.

It was a blast Anderson said would have traveled 480 feet had it not been for the gale blowing in. That homer was Hollywood stuff, and it seemed to win over Detroit's baseball fans in a big way.

Many figured Kirk Gibson was growing up as a professional ballplayer, as I was named Detroit Baseball Writers 1981 Tiger of the Year. It looked like the Tigers and I were ready for a great 1982 season.

Instead, 1982 was nothing but trouble. I ended up playing in only 69 games, thanks to a barrage of injuries: knee, calf, and again the same wrist I had hurt in 1980. For toppers, I lost 15 pounds in 2½ weeks during May to an illness they spent days trying to diagnose. Not until they treated me for Giardia—an intestinal parasite that robs you of nutrition—did I get better.

I had gone into a quick 3-for-35 April slump, during which I badly bruised my knee in Kansas City. Then, later on, I got into a bad flap in New York with Sparky that did me no good at all. I made a couple of bad plays in the outfield, and our trainer, Pio DiSalvo, told Anderson that I was limping badly and needed to come out as we tried to hold off the Yankees in the seventh inning.

Sparky waved me off the field as he brought in a defensive replacement—during the game—so I just waved right on back. I wanted to be there when it counted, and I wasn't going to come out with the game on the line.

Finally, with the game being delayed, very reluctantly, and very angrily, I made my way back to the dugout. I smashed my sunglasses against a wall and threw a tantrum. Now, it was the manager who felt he had been shown up, and I deserved an earful.

"I am the *law!* I am the *ruler!*" he told the media afterward, still raging, and pretty much giving them the same message he had given me. "I learned a long time ago not to care about what my players think."

I realized instantly who had been out of line, and I made sure the press understood that I backed my manager fully. I realized I had to learn to control my emotions. Though sometimes it could not be helped—such as the "brawlgame" we hosted in mid-May against the Twins at Tiger Stadium. It got started

WHEN I FIRST PLAYED FOR SPARKY, HE TOLD ME I HAD TO PACE MYSELF OR ELSE MY BODY WOULD BREAK. I TOLD HIM I COULDN'T COMPROMISE MY WAY OF PERFORMING, AND ADDED, "IF I BREAK, THEY CAN FIX ME."

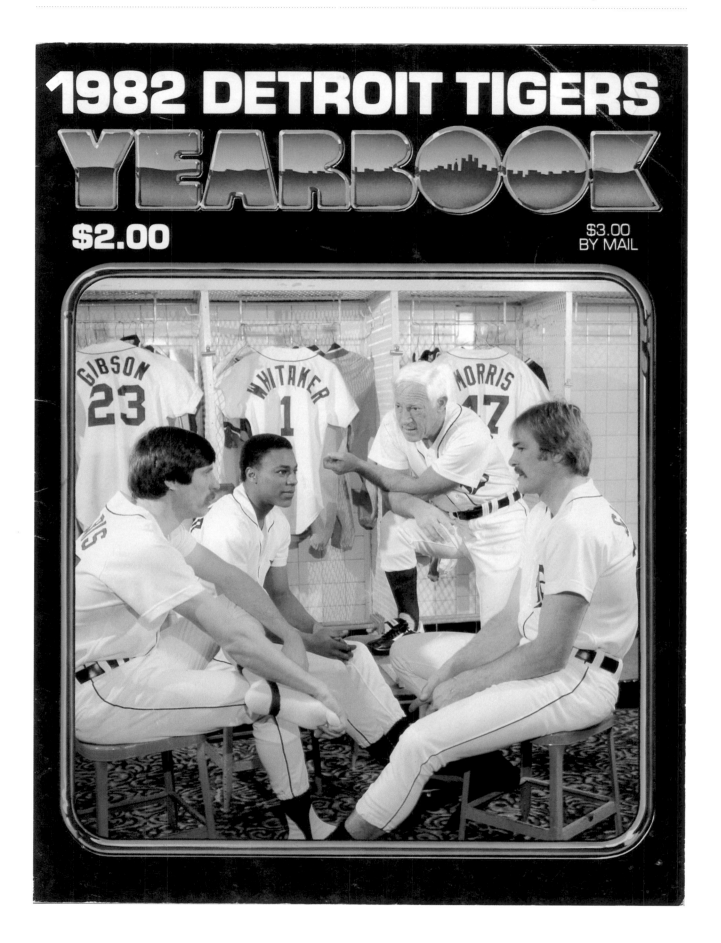

early when Pete Redfern hit Chet Lemon with a pitch. The dugouts emptied when Chet went after Redfern, and Chet and Jim Lemon, Minnesota's pitching coach, got tossed, along with Billy Gardner, the Twins manager.

With bad blood pushing the tension higher and higher, extra innings can make tempers quickly re-ignite. Sure enough, we got locked up in a 2–2 doozy, and in the 10th inning Ron Davis, the Twins reliever, threw a ball that nearly hit Larry Herndon in the head.

In the 11th the final fuse was lit. With the score still tied, Davis clipped Enos Cabell with a pitch, and all hell broke loose. Enos went for Davis, I ended up wrestling for a moment with Minnesota's catcher, Sal Butera, and everyone stormed the infield as the umpires tried to settle things down.

I stomped to the mound and really began giving it to Davis: "What a derelict! What an idiot! As hard as you throw the ball, you're going to fire one at his head? Is that ever weak!"

Right then, out of the corner of my eye, I spotted Twins infielder Jesùs Vega getting ready to sucker-punch me in the side of the head. I ducked, and his punch caught Richie Hebner square in the ear, which re-ignited the melee.

We disintegrated into a punching, fist-swinging swarm of alley-fighters that moved from the infield area clear across the

Never willing to back down, here with Milwaukee's Robin Yount

diamond to the Twins dugout. It was out of control, with guys squaring off all over the place.

Breaking up a double play—my way.

The guy who got the worst of it was Dave Rozema, who tried karate-kicking John Castino and tore ligaments in his knee, finishing him for the season. Seven players ended up getting tossed out that night, and the only good thing that happened was that two batters later I drilled a home run and we won, 4–2. I had five hits that night, and Rozie was the winning pitcher, but what I loved about it, beyond winning a game so ugly, was that a developing baseball team had decided—together—that we would do what it took to win.

I wish the good times could have lasted, but I sprained my wrist early in July and went on the disabled list July 15, joining Rozema on the sidelines for the remainder of the season. The only headlines we now began to generate in 1982 were the kind he and I didn't need—in the gossip columns.

This led to Sparky's speech concluding the 1982 season at the Detroit Baseball Writers dinner—a speech I didn't understand at the time. Believing that I was heading downward, he spoke of—without once mentioning my name—the need for players to be polite and to sign autographs, to appreciate their positions, and to be grateful for the attention of fans.

This philosophy might be great for Sparky, but it wasn't for Kirk Gibson.

CHAPTER *seven*

I HAD HIT ROCK BOTTOM. I HAD SUFFERED THROUGH A YEAR WHEN EVEN THE THOUGHT OF GOING TO TIGER STADIUM MADE ME SICK, AND THOUGH I DIDN'T HAVE AN ANSWER THAT MIGHT END MY MISERY, I KNEW I COULD NOT GO THROUGH ANOTHER SEASON LIKE THAT.

Two months after I closed out an ugly 1983 season during which I had only hit .227 and been an all-around flop, I drove to a friend's Lapeer, Michigan, farm where I kept my horse, Rusty. It was the beginning of December, with the Christmas season arriving—a time when I'm normally at my best.

It was a cold, windy day with snowflakes cutting the air as I saddled Rusty. I wore a fringed leather jacket and a cowboy hat that could never have protected me from the chill. Maybe, deep down, I wanted to be exposed.

My best friend, a golden retriever named Nick, tromped along with us as we rode for two hours through woodlots and among bare trees that swayed in the raw December wind. In a setting so lonely, here was a place to strip away years of protective veneer that I had built up, and to begin addressing a few basic truths. I knew that I was a jerk, and that my life was out of control.

We pulled up high atop a hill. I sat on Rusty, facing dead into the wind and snow, with Nick next to us. They seemed to sense my desperation.

For too long I had been fooling myself, like a hunter lost in the woods who's certain he's headed north. After hiking for two hours, he checks his compass, discovers he's walking dead south, and panic sets in. I was no less lost, and no less scared. I was ready to give up on my baseball career and abandon my dream. But as I looked into Nick's eyes and felt Rusty's warmth, I knew I had to change. Suddenly I felt inspired to fight on. To be calm, and not panic. To think it out and make the right decision. I had to find an answer. I had to change my life.

After a few more minutes I headed down the hill, Nick bounding alongside. We got back to the barn and in out of the wind. I dried Rusty off, my mind whirling and adrenaline rushing. A life and a career had sunk far enough. It was time for a turnaround. I went into the house, grabbed the telephone, dialed my agent in Seattle, Doug Baldwin, and said:

"I can't handle this any more. I've got to get some help."

My call was the equivalent of an alcoholic deciding to go to his first AA meeting. I was desperate, but Doug knew, as did everyone close to me, that nothing would change until I personally came to grips with, and acknowledged, a disintegrating life.

"If I can make a suggestion," he said, "I know these people out here."

He recommended a place called the Pacific Institute, a kind of Seattle-based clinic for the mind and soul. I flew there immediately and met with an Italian gentleman named Frank

Bartenetti. From the moment I met him, I sensed an aura about him, something that commanded respect. It didn't come from the intimidation I'd been used to in the sports world, but from a projection of his own inner confidence. It impressed me.

We talked things out, and he helped me focus on some basic issues—who I was, who I wanted to be, what I wanted to accomplish, and how to secure the life I wanted by changing my thought processes. In short, how to get out of the negative world I was living in. For four days, Frank gave me a one-on-one seminar that turned my life around. The Pacific Institute promoted a long line of psychological concepts: accountability, goal setting, and changing comfort zones to control your subconscious, which controls you.

By regulating your subconscious, you could prearrange success, or ensure failure, all depending on the level at which you see yourself. I had seen myself as a failure, and my subconscious had kept me there. I had been accepting defeat.

Take, for example, people who are not comfortable in public speaking situations. Subconsciously, they do not believe they're good public speakers, therefore they approach the microphone and instantly communicate—by way of a quavering voice, nervous gestures, etcetera—that they are not good on their feet. It's a self-fulfilling mindset.

The golf course is another glowing illustration: You have never in your life broken 80 for 18 holes. You see yourself shooting in the 80s. You've played 17 holes and are on the 18th tee, when your opponent points out that you only have to make a 6 on the final hole—an easy par 4—to post your best score, a 79. You promptly fall apart, making an 8 to shoot 81. It is a prearranged failure—your subconscious controlling you. Instead, what you must do is envision yourself birdieing the last hole to shoot 76. Then you will succeed.

The same tussles with prearranged failure can crop up in baseball and in everyday life, which is where they were occurring for me throughout 1983. I had to learn to handle these situations by changing my comfort zone. I had to make a conscious effort to control which thoughts I allowed into my mind, because those thoughts would subconsciously affect my actions.

It would require almost a complete reversal from the way I had been thinking—and acting.

"I can't," I told Bartenetti, figuring my habits were too ingrained.

"You mean you won't," he corrected. "You're off your track. You have the power to change. Don't panic. I'll show you how to think and act properly."

In 1983 my thought processes had become increasingly negative. When coming to bat in the bottom of the ninth, with the game on the line and a tough pitcher on the mound, I would say to myself, "My God, this guy is nasty. I don't want to make the last out of the game. I don't want to strike out."

It was like filing a flight plan for disaster. If success occurred in such a situation, it was purely by accident.

Bartenetti taught me to react differently. Radically so. Now, if I struck out in a key situation, I would say to myself, "That's not like me," and I would begin to imprint a positive image in my mind, rubbing out the old one. The way to turn those negative scenarios around, as I learned at the Pacific Institute, was to change my personal comfort zone through *affirmation and visualization.*

"I love pressure situations. I perform even better under these circumstances." There's the affirmation. Now, I follow up with the visualization. I see myself in a packed stadium with the game on the line hitting a home run off Goose Gossage to win the game. I can visualize such a moment very clearly.

It's part of the basic Pacific Institute formula: I x V = R.
Image times vividness equals reality.

The more vividly I envision myself or an event, the more likely it is to become reality.

Bartenetti had me visualizing and affirming every morning when I got up and every night when I went to bed. After four days in Seattle, I now had a different blueprint for living my life. Weak habits—both personally and professionally—were on the wane. A new attitude was on the rise. I had not felt this good since my days at Michigan State.

I still faced a lot of work, beginning with tuning my body toward higher performance. I stuck to a workout regimen every bit as fierce as that summer I had experienced before my freshman year at MSU. I was on the weight machines, I swam, ran, pruned my diet and dropped 15 pounds, visualizing a new Kirk Gibson.

As miserable as I had been in 1983, I had a complete turn-around in '84. When I walked into spring training in early February, everyone saw it. I was clean-shaven—no long hair and no three-day beard. I was tuned, mentally and physically, and ready to take no prisoners. I was a new man—a new person—and I was going to play every game with the fire and intensity I had visualized over the winter. I was going to be a champion. I was focused. I was smiling and enjoying life. Everyone on the team was watching me closely, and what they noticed is that now, when I did say something, there was a new and focused intensity, reflective of a new man, and a new ballplayer.

The Tigers had wanted me at the end of the '83 season to play winter ball and learn to play first base, but I had told them

> **THE BASIC PACIFIC INSTITUTE FORMULA: I X V = R. IMAGE TIMES VIVIDNESS EQUALS REALITY.**

Kaline 101.

to forget it. I had needed to get away from baseball. Now I was showing the benefits.

To help me become a better right fielder, the Tigers set me up to work directly with Al Kaline, the great Hall of Fame right fielder who had played 21 years in Detroit. It was a great move.

Recognizing quickly that I was better at charging in on the ball, rather than going back on the ball, Kaline wanted me to play deeper in the outfield. He also showed me how to position myself to avoid the blinding sun in Tiger Stadium's right field, which gave me fits, but had never seemed to be a problem for him.

Kaline changed my throwing mechanics as well. He taught me to throw with a cross-seam grip, with more of an overhand motion, and to pull straight down on the ball. This would keep the ball from tailing away, which for too long had been a bad habit of mine.

Kaline hit me thousands of balls during outfield practice. Bag after bag after bag. He always stopped to demonstrate the proper technique. On the eve of turning 50, he still moved as effortlessly as he had during his playing days.

I lacked his level of skill and grace, but he never lost patience with me—never yelled, never screamed. After I had messed one up, he always corrected me with an even voice, saying, "Gibby, try fielding it this way." He was a Hall of Famer in all respects, and through him I developed a confidence and a capability brand new to me and to the Tigers.

Before, I would check the weather on a day when I knew I would be playing right field at Tiger Stadium. Bright sunshine would lead to instant dejection. I automatically anticipated trouble. Now, thanks to my winter training and to Kaline's lessons, I was visualizing and affirming that I could play right field. So, too, were the Tigers. They dealt Glenn Wilson and John Wockenfuss to Philadelphia for the prized relief pitcher, Willie Hernandez, and for a smooth first baseman and pinch-hitter named Dave Bergman. I knew of Hernandez's reputation, just as I knew we needed a late-innings fireman to help out our regular right-handed ace, Aurelio Lopez. Even better, Hernandez was a lefty.

It had the earmarks of a terrific trade, especially after Hernandez drove over from Clearwater, put on his Tiger uniform, and in his first inning of work for us, gunned down three batters on nine pitches.

After spring training, Roger Craig, our pitching coach, picked up where Kaline left off. He had seen enough of me to recognize that I was going to be a major contributor in 1984, and started lobbying Sparky Anderson to make me our every-day right fielder. At a time when I still had to re-earn Anderson's confidence, Craig would half-kid to Sparky that if I didn't play every day, he would quit.

"Hey, man, I want you out there as our starting right fielder!" he would say to me, making me feel like a Marine ready to hit the beach. "Gibby, we're going to practice every day. I'll hit you balls every day. You're my guy. You need to be playing every day."

As many balls as Kaline hit to me during spring training, during the season Craig matched it and then some, as we worked together, separate from his time with the pitchers. Roger Craig became for me the perfect complement to my time at the Pacific Institute. He was a nonstop source for positive thoughts, and all those fly balls and hot grounders he hit at me turned me into the capable right fielder who would make plays that season that I could never have dreamed of making before.

All we knew coming north, out of spring training and into the real season in 1984, was that we should be contenders. We had good starting pitching—Jack Morris, Dan Petry, Milt Wilcox—

and we had an awesome 1–2 bullpen punch of Lopez and Hernandez. We were strong as steel up the middle, with Lance Parrish catching, Alan Trammell and Lou Whitaker at shortstop and second base, and Chet Lemon in center. We had added an excellent power hitter during the off-season when Detroit signed Darrell Evans.

Evans was the final piece that turned us into a *great* team. He led us with talks in the clubhouse hours after the game. We talked about strategy, key moments, pitches, and plays that had been made. We reviewed what had worked and what hadn't, and then we prepared for the next game, discussing the opposing pitcher and team and what we needed to do to beat them. It was an education that only a veteran with Evans' experience could provide.

At the time, it was the greatest think-tank I had experienced in sports. And all because it was centered entirely around the players controlling our team's destiny. In the process we wrote the book on how good teams police themselves.

If someone did something ignorant, it was brought up and handled immediately. It was constructive criticism in a way that made us better as a team.

It was the atmosphere in which winning becomes habit. We began the 1984 season with an opening sweep at Minnesota, then moved on to Chicago for another sweep that featured Morris throwing a no-hitter. Then it was home for a cleanup of the Rangers, with Evans hitting an Opening Day home run on his first swing at Tiger Stadium.

The pattern never seemed to change. Whitaker would get a leadoff hit, Trammell would follow with a single, or a double into the corner, and then someone batting in the middle of the lineup—either Evans, Parrish, or myself—would get an extra-base hit or a home run, and we would be up, 2–0, 3–0, 4–0, in the first inning.

If we needed a homer late in the game off a tough guy like Dan Quisenberry of the Royals, we would get one, even if a player such as Alan Trammell or Tommy Brookens, who weren't by trade big home run hitters, had to park one.

When we got into the late innings with a lead, it was curtains for the opposition: Lopez would help finish things off by torching teams in the seventh and eighth, leaving the mop-up for Hernandez and his awesome screwball, which in 1984 was untouchable.

On top of all that, we even had bench players who could come through in the clutch. A perfect example of this was Dave Bergman, who filled in at first base and as a pinch-hitter. He might have had one of the best at-bats ever during a televised

WELCOME TO TIGERTOWN – ROARING IN '84

Crossing the Canadian border into Detroit, 1984.

Monday night game in June. The Blue Jays, who had stubbornly been keeping the heat on us after our great start, were in town for a huge series, and, as usual, Tiger Stadium was packed and the night was electric.

We were tied in the ninth. Bergie came on to pinch-hit against a tough Blue Jays right-hander, Roy Lee Jackson. They ground each other to a 3-and-2 count, then Bergman fouled off seven consecutive pitches in an intense confrontation between the two men.

Finally, Bergie drilled a knee-high fastball into the right field upper deck. The crowd went wild.

Destiny. Six weeks into the season we were 35–5.

We were the hottest story in sports. We were on the cover of *Sports Illustrated*. The *New York Times*, *The Sporting News*—every major media outlet wanted a story, and reporters stood four deep around our lockers. We were *the* sports story of 1984.

We set Detroit afire during an '84 season in which we won 104 games and led the American League East Division from the first day until the last. It was crazy in Detroit and around Michigan. The crowds. The attention. Songs and slogans blaring on local TV and radio. Our Detroit Tigers network TV ratings were out of sight. People could not get enough of us.

I finished with a .282 batting average, with 27 home runs, 91 RBIs, and 29 stolen bases. I actually looked forward to going to the ballpark, which was a total reversal from the horror story I had lived only a year earlier.

We clinched the American League East Division and roared into the playoffs against Kansas City. We knew what baseball's best team was obliged to do. And we expected to win.

Any player who has appeared in a League Championship or World Series game knows there is a tremendous sense of tension. Every game. Every play. Every pitch is crucial. Any play can make the difference between winning or losing—and you don't know which one it might be, so with each pitch you hold your breath in anticipation. That's why, once the competition is finished, and you've won, there is such indescribable elation. And if you win the League Championship, the intensity is taken to an even higher level for the World Series.

Kansas City was our first hurdle. We had endured a few pains at Royals Stadium over the years, but Trammell had a triple and a home run in Game One, while Morris pitched a five-hitter, and we won, 8–1.

The best help I could have provided came on defense in the third inning, with us leading, 2–0. George Brett ripped a bases-loaded drive that would have slammed into the right field corner and cleared the bases had I not been able to gallop over and glove it.

"I thought he was crazy to even try for it," Brett said after the game.

Sparky shook his head. "A year ago," he said, "Gibson wouldn't have gotten that ball."

Compliments on a defensive effort? Things really had changed.

Game Two was a classic display of our depth. I hit a home run and Johnny Grubb hammered a deep two-run double in the 11th inning, as we won, 5–3. Then, in Game Three, Wilcox pitched two-hit ball. Hernandez finished off, and we won, 1–0, to head into the World Series, and our final hurdle.

We waited at home on the Sunday before the Series began, our bags packed, not knowing if we would be playing Chicago or San Diego. When the Padres came back in Game Five to win and sweep the final three games of the series, we headed west to play a dangerous club that had just ambushed the Cubs.

We got the kind of jump on San Diego we had gotten on teams the entire season:

Game One: Larry Herndon hit a two-run homer and Morris went all the way. We won, 3–2. I made Kaline proud by helping gun down Kurt Bevacqua at third base in the seventh inning. He had tried to stretch a double into a triple, but a perfect relay to Whitaker from deep in the right field corner nailed him.

"KIRK GIBSON RAISED EVERYBODY ELSE'S PERFORMANCE TO ANOTHER LEVEL. HE DEMANDED THAT OF YOU IF YOU WERE HIS TEAMMATE, AND I THINK THAT'S WHAT MOST EVERYBODY RESPECTS."

—Lance Parrish

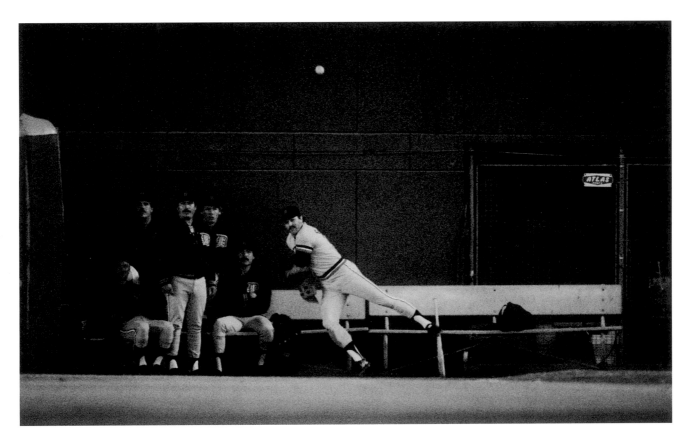

A good relay to nail Bevacqua for a big out.

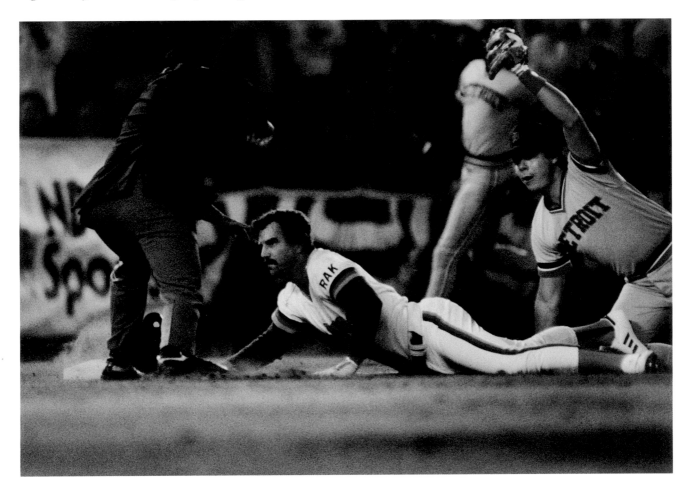

Game 5—my first home run.

Game Two: Bevacqua got his revenge, hitting a three-run homer, then raising his fist and blowing kisses as he rounded the bases. That pushed our desire to win even higher. Unfortunately, Andy Hawkins went on to shut us down in middle relief after we had taken a quick 3–0 lead, and San Diego won, 5–3.

Game Three: San Diego walked 11 batters, which tied a World Series record. Marty Castillo, my Class A Lakeland Tigers teammate and another of our quality part-timers, hit a two-run homer. We won, 5–2.

Game Four: Showtime for Trammell, who hit two home runs, and in the process got some of the national attention and respect he deserved. Morris pitched a five-hitter. We took a 3–1 Series lead with a 4–2 victory.

We came to the ballpark for Game Five on a gray, gloomy Sunday in Detroit. The atmosphere, though, was electric. The fans,

Aggressive play on the base paths.

sensing a world championship that had eluded Detroit for 16 years, were pumped. So was I. I wanted to finish off the Padres now, and not mess around with any sixth or seventh games.

We ripped into Mark Thurmond in the first inning for three runs, two of them on a breaking pitch I slammed for a home run into the upper deck in right center field. San Diego came back and tied it in the fourth, 3–3. In the next inning, I was on third base with one out when Rusty Kuntz came on to pinch-hit against Craig Lefferts. He hit a pop-up to shallow right field that the Padres' second baseman, Alan Wiggins, backpedaled on and caught just into the outfield grass. His momentum carried him away from home plate, making it impossible to make a strong throw home.

I had no business tagging at third, but it was my football instinct, driving me to put all the heat on an opponent. By tagging up on a ball hit so shallow, I had the advantage in that I was hitting the opposing team with a huge element of surprise. Even if the throw was there, I was fully prepared to level their catcher, Terry Kennedy, as hard as I had drilled Tommy Graves during a football scrimmage nine years earlier.

It was a calculated decision, a chance in my mind to win the game. The throw never reached home plate, and I slid so fiercely that I ripped the knee out of my uniform pants.

Lance Parrish hit a hard line drive home run in the seventh to make it a 5–3 game, then the Padres got one back in the eighth. It was now 5–4 in the bottom of the eighth when I got a chance to bat against my old rival, Goose Gossage, with runners at second and third, and one out.

Dick Williams, the Padres manager, was going to make the obvious move, with first base open, and walk me intentionally. But Gossage shook him off. He knew he had owned me since my first night in the majors, and he was chalking up Gibson as one more strikeout.

Williams walked to the mound to get things straight. I stood watching their debate, and then I looked back into the dugout at Sparky, who flashed four fingers. He figured along with everyone else that the Padres had to walk me.

But Gossage would not allow it. Strikeout after strikeout, he had tortured me for years, and he wasn't backing away now. I looked back toward the dugout as Williams and Gossage jawed. I yelled to Sparky, "Ten bucks says they pitch to me and I crank it." He broke into a little half-smile.

Gossage got his way and was standing on the mound ready for me. I walked from the on-deck circle to home plate. The crowd noise built to a feverish pitch, anticipating this heavyweight clash, as I affirmed to myself, "I love pressure situations."

I tapped home plate with my bat and took a couple of quick half-cuts. Gossage had abused me for the last time. His decision to pitch was a flagrant declaration of supremacy. But he wasn't going to win. Not here. Not now, not in front of my family, my

I JUST BATTLE. THAT'S MY ASSET. THAT'S THE BEST THING I HAVE TO OFFER—A STRONG DESIRE AND DETERMINATION TO GET THE JOB DONE. THAT TRANSLATES INTO GAMES YOU WIN THAT YOU'RE NOT SUPPOSED TO.

Gossage unloads another fastball.

Sweet revenge.

friends, 50,000 roaring Tiger fans—not before millions watching this showdown on television.

"It's out of here," I visualized, the image bright and bold in my mind.

Gossage went into his routine, and it was the same stage play all over again. He just shook his head, cranked up, and blistered a fastball that was off the plate. Ball one.

Gossage reared back and delivered another screaming fastball. This time it was my turn. The ball exploded off my bat, rocketing on a line deep into the upper-deck seats in right field.

I can remember the thunder of the crowd as the ball disappeared into the sea of screaming fans. I remember the feeling of triumph, of having rid myself of all the past ugliness, as I trotted around the bases on the sweetest victory lap imaginable. The game was over. The World Series was ours. They knew it. We knew it. Everyone knew it.

I almost killed some of our guys with high fives as I crossed home plate. I couldn't contain myself as I turned toward the dugout, feeling the emotions from the crowd, and, really, from an entire baseball city. I took a giant-sized, celebratory leap that was captured by *Detroit Free Press* photographer Mary

Saluting those who never left me.

Schroeder (on cover). It captured in that instant all of the excitement, the intensity, the desire, and the commitment to be a World Champion.

San Diego went calmly in the ninth, and Detroit got on with a party it had been waiting for 16 years to throw.

I went home and joined my whole family in a personal celebration a few hours after we had spilled the last of our clubhouse champagne. They knew more than anyone else what had gone into making this day, this year, this brand new life.

Dave Rozema and I savor the moment.

The fruits of victory.

CHAPTER *eight*

FOLLOWING A WINTER OF APPEARANCES, HONORS, AND CELE-
BRATIONS, EVERYONE FIGURED WE WOULD COME TO FLORIDA IN
FEBRUARY OF 1985 STILL GLOWING FROM OUR WORLD SERIES
GLORY. PEOPLE WHO THOUGHT I MIGHT SHOW UP AT SPRING TRAINING
GRACIOUS AND SATISFIED QUICKLY TOOK A FEW STEPS BACK AS THEY ARRIVED AT MY LOCKER IN OUR
CLUBHOUSE AT MARCHANT STADIUM. I HAD STUCK A SIGN ON MY CUBICLE THAT READ: I'M ORNERY.

Getting into the right frame of mind to repeat as world champions is one of the most difficult feats in sports. I intended to play with as much fury in 1985 as I had during our world championship season the year before. The message attached to my locker was part of my competitive philosophy, which I explained during an interview with Booth Newspapers:

"The sticker signifies that I'm not on the field to make friends. I want to win in any way that's legal, and it's legal to go into second base and drill the SOB so his relay goes into the dugout."

I had never liked the chumminess that seemed to exist between too many opposing players. There was too much buddy-buddy chatter around the batting cages. Too many smiles and conversations on the base paths.

I had told more than one guy I played with, "You want to be friends with so-and-so, fine. Go take him to dinner for all I care. Just don't do it in front of me."

Sometimes I was even nastier with my teammates. There was a day during spring training when Jack Morris had gotten showy about his leisurely routine. He would sometimes do his conditioning, shower up, and head out the door at 10:15 a.m., while the rest of the team was just getting into the thick of workouts.

"I'm going fishing today," he would say, rubbing in the fact that his every-other-day throwing schedule gave him a certain amount of latitude. As he would head out the door at mid-morning, we might hear, "I'm going pig hunting today," which meant he was off to some game ranch to hunt wild pigs.

My teammates were getting miffed at the way he was flaunting his freedom. Darrell Evans said something to him, which was Evans' role as unofficial Team Dad, and when Jack gave him some back talk, I got into Jack's face.

"Hey, I've had enough of your act," I told him. "We're busting our tails and you're going hunting. We don't appreciate your flaunting. Change right now or you'll get hurt." He immediately realized it didn't need to go any further.

It wasn't as rough as it sounds, though. Jack was family, and this was the way our clubhouse family policed itself. It was the way that Darrell, in his own dignified way, had motivated

1984 World Series parade.

us to handle problems that could affect team relations and performance.

I loved it. I didn't believe in saying something behind a guy's back. If there was a problem, I had no qualms about bringing it up, face to face. It took the edge off any situation—quickly.

We had other occasional problems with players who happened to be hurt, or ill, at the most coincidental of times. "Your toe hurts? Not feeling well? No chance it has anything to do with the fact that Nolan Ryan's pitching tonight—does it?"

"Ryanitis," we called it, and certain players seemed quite susceptible to this disease.

I recall an occasion in Toronto when Chet Lemon had been hurt for some time, and yet his injury didn't seem to be causing any undue misery as he took two hours of early batting practice. A while later, we heard, "I can't play tonight."

It was a day or two later, and I knew Chet had "recovered" and was back in the lineup. I hollered at Billy Consolo, the official lineup reader, to read the lineup for us. It started off, as usual, with Consolo reading, "Leading off, Lou Whitaker...batting second, Alan Trammel..." Until he got to Chet: "...batting eighth, Chet Lemon."

"WHO? WHO'S THE NEW GUY? WOW! NICE TO SEE YOU COULD MAKE IT BACK, CHET!" I interrupted, hollering across the clubhouse.

Lemon got into his defensive mode and brushed off the jibes.

"Aw, Gibby, man, that's weak."

"It's about time," I said.

"Well, what are you saying? You saying that I'm jaking you guys?"

I was being playful as opposed to hostile, but the message was clear.

"I'm telling you that's *exactly* what the boys think."

"Awww, bull," and he walked away. But Chet knew. It had gone too far, and we expected him to suck it up.

Player commitment, though, was not our problem as 1985 began unfolding. Everyone was figuring a young bunch of world champions, just hitting their prime, would probably be contending for a repeat. I still can't explain what happened, except that, from the start, things never clicked like they had in 1984.

I had a tough at-bat against Oakland in the early weeks that sort of typified our year. I was batting against Tim Birtsas, a big left-hander from Clarkston, Michigan—right next door to the community in which I had grown up. In fact, I had helped recruit Birtsas to play baseball at Michigan State.

In the third inning of a game at Tiger Stadium, with one out and the bases loaded, Birtsas let loose with a high fastball that ran in on me and smashed me in the mouth.

There was an immediate blast of sensations—numbness, then pain—as I began poking at my mouth, probing for missing

The only time I was ejected in the American League.

A shot to the mouth sent me reeling and resulted in 17 stitches.

teeth. Then our trainer, Pio DiSalvo, arrived. Amid the pain, I had no patience.

"Let me see," he said.

"What's there to see? Do I have any teeth?"

"Yeah."

"OK, then let me go to first base," I mumbled, with my mouth swelling up, "I'll run the bases and we'll go get it stitched up."

There wasn't any martyrdom involved. I was bleeding, but if my teeth were in place the other stuff could certainly wait until the inning was wrapped up.

At that moment I turned around and saw a couple of middle-aged women sitting in front-row box seats. When they got a look at my mouth, each of them broke into an ugly, contorted expression, and that's when I knew my mouth must be a mess.

I ended up leaving the ballgame for a visit to the hospital that was worth 17 stitches. My face was puffed up, purple, and stitched, and by the next morning I looked like a bad Halloween mask. I got to the ballpark and Sparky Anderson had dropped me from the lineup. I went directly into his office.

"Hey, Skip, what's going on here?"

"Gibby," he said, "you've got to take some time off from that thing."

Sparky Anderson taught me and my teammates in the early 80s the game of baseball—how it was to be played and how to respect it. He preached professionalism, though it took some time for me to understand that. He molded our team. When we played teams like the Orioles—who knew the fundamentals that make your team successful—and they executed the right play, he would say, "See, that is how the game is played." The next day, we would be practicing the very same play.

He was the ruler. He was the manager. We were the players—nothing else.

If as manager he asked us to do something in a game, and we failed, and looked stupid trying it, he would always defend us in the paper as carrying out his decision. He had few team meetings, but a couple come to mind.

He preached to us about his "garden," and how he liked his garden to grow great vegetables. And the only way he could do that was to make sure there were no weeds in that garden. If he found a weed, he would tell us, while looking at a specific player, "I'll take it out." Soon thereafter, you knew that player was gone.

Another was his "Cinderella's slipper" story. He would walk out in the middle of the club-house, take his slippers off, and put them in the middle of the floor. He would then walk around the room, talking to us about some things he didn't like going on. Walking back to his shoes, he'd point at them and say, "These are Cinderella's slippers. Walk by, and if they fit, just get right on your horse and ride on out of here, because nobody's going to miss you."

I respect Sparky most because he always allowed me to come into his office, close the door behind me, and speak my mind—whether it was warranted, or emotional or irrelevant. Not interrupting me, he would always say after I was done, "Thank you, Mr. Gibson," waving me out softly with his hand toward the door. I knew, whether I was right or wrong, he always thought about what was said. What more can you ask from a human being?

The truth was, there was nothing seriously wrong with me. I looked bad, and my mouth hurt, but it was a long way from the kind of injury that should keep a person out of the lineup. To me, it wasn't just a matter of wanting to play, but an issue of personal credibility. A guy who considered himself a team leader, a person who had little patience with players who yielded to small injuries, needed to show his leadership by playing.

Sparky put me back into the lineup that night against California, and in the first inning, I hit a home run off Kirk McCaskill that landed in the upper-deck bleachers in right center field. Unfortunately, after the home run, I went into something like a 2–for–40 slump, which had nothing to do with a sore mouth and everything to do with bad hitting.

It seemed as if everyone on our team was just having an average season as '85 unfolded. We were somehow missing the magic. Toronto was tearing apart our division, and we were hovering just above .500. It wasn't pretty, and no matter what we tried, it didn't work. We finished the year 15 games out of first place. Even after winning it all in 1984, I never fully realized what a feat it was to be world champions until we didn't repeat in 1985.

I almost left Detroit at the end of 1985, but signed a three-year extension a minute before the contract deadline. After my big year in 1984, I had decided to gamble and play out my option in 1985, then take a shot at free agency following the '85 season. It looked as if my timing would be perfect.

I would also be making a tremendous change in my personal life—a very positive one. I married JoAnn Sklarski on December 21, 1985, in a double-ring ceremony with Dave Rozema and JoAnn's sister, Sandy. Of course, the wedding had the media working overtime, but all that mattered to me was that, in

Signing my three-year extension in 1986.

JoAnn, I had found serenity and happiness that I had never known before. There was a shift in my priorities toward a new sacrifice and a new commitment. I had found the right person, and it was time to start a family.

I was having entirely different feelings about the free-agent market, however, which had become another version of The Big Chill. I was supposedly baseball's most eligible free agent, but I was getting nowhere, as one club after another began dropping out of the bidding. The Chicago Cubs, Los Angeles Dodgers, Atlanta Braves, New York Yankees—every team that had called me for a meeting to discuss playing for them had, within 24 hours, called and backed out.

Sports Illustrated put me on its cover with the heading: "HARD TIME FOR FREE AGENTS," beneath which was a sub-title: "Kirk Gibson—the Superstar No One Wants."

The cold-shouldering was later determined by a federal arbitrator, Tom Roberts, to have been pure collusion—a con-spiracy against free agents. The Tigers had dropped from serious

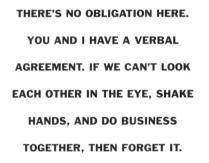

THERE'S NO OBLIGATION HERE.

YOU AND I HAVE A VERBAL

AGREEMENT. IF WE CAN'T LOOK

EACH OTHER IN THE EYE, SHAKE

HANDS, AND DO BUSINESS

TOGETHER, THEN FORGET IT.

—Kirk Gibson,
on how his 15-year deal with agent,
Doug Baldwin, started

consideration because of their refusal to discuss anything beyond a three-year deal, a demand I thought was reasonable because of my young age and my production during '84 and '85. Unfortunately, I turned this tense contract negotiation into a media disaster when, in declining the Tigers' offer, I chose the following words: "I would vomit if I were forced to sign a three-year deal with Detroit." It received an appropriate response from the Tiger fans.

While on our honeymoon, after making occasional calls to my agent, Doug Baldwin, my choices were clear. At 11:59 p.m. on January 8, 1986, one minute before the deadline—and with no other offers—I signed the three-year deal with Detroit.

I felt no bitterness as I reported to spring training in February of 1986. In fact, I felt great. I was happily married, and ready for a big season at an age when many players hit their prime. I had rarely sensed as much command at the plate, and it showed from the first day. Al Kaline paid me a nice compliment when he told the papers that I was the smartest hitter on the team at setting up pitchers.

I had gotten off to a terrific start early in the '86 season and was feeling good as we began a short series at Fenway Park against the Boston Red Sox. In the first inning of the series opener, I managed a walk from Roger Clemens. Leading off at first, I shot back to the bag as Clemens threw to the first baseman.

A bit of Boston trivia is that Fenway Park was notorious for having bad bases. Some areas of the bags were firm, others were soft. On this particular night they were also wet from an earlier ground crew spraying. My foot first hit a harder portion of the bag, then slid because of the moisture until my spikes caught on a softer area, which caused my foot and ankle to twist at an unnatural angle.

Clemens said afterward, "From the pitcher's mound I heard a popping noise. I knew he was messed up, either broken or a bad sprain."

Sharing a special moment.

Boston in 1986.

I missed the next 6 weeks. My next game wasn't until June 2.

We finished only 8½ games behind the Red Sox, who came within a botched ground ball of winning the World Series.

In 1987 we started off with a big loss before the season even started. Lance Parrish, our All-star Catcher, didn't like his negotiations with the Tigers and signed a free-agent contract with the Philadelphia Phillies. Not only was Parrish a good player, but he was a great influence on our team. He would be impossible to replace on both counts.

On the field, 1987 started like 1986. We were getting ready to break camp in Lakeland and head north when, on a rainy, windy day, we moved indoors for batting practice. I stepped into the cage, took a swing, and dropped to the ground as if I had been shot. I couldn't breathe. It was such a routine swing that the guys thought I was screwing around as I rolled on the ground with pain. It turned out to be a torn rib muscle that would put me on the shelf for the first month of the season.

With Parrish gone, and with me on the disabled list through April, we got off to a lousy start, and remained buried at the bottom of our division well into May. Sparky Anderson then said publicly that we would end up surprising everyone by becoming serious contenders.

Sparky knew what he was talking about. We went 89–49 the rest of the way, and got into a dandy divisional race with Toronto. We also picked up a couple of players—Doyle Alexander and Bill Madlock—who made a huge difference as we went into the August-September stretch. Unfortunately, to get Alexander we had to give up John Smoltz, who later went on to win the Cy Young Award at Atlanta.

Alexander was a strike-throwing right-hander who had a reputation as being a dour kind of leave-me-alone guy. He was just that—a pure gamer who wanted to do his job and be left alone. It was an intensity level that I fully appreciated, and he finished 10–0 for us, keeping us in the hunt.

We were chasing the Blue Jays as we headed into the final two weekends of the '87 season, with a four-game series set in Toronto, to be followed by a season-closing three-game duel in Detroit. With 10 days remaining, we were trailing the first-place Jays by a half-game when we arrived at Exhibition Stadium. They beat us Thursday night, beat us in extra innings on Friday night, and then topped us again in extra innings on Saturday. In both extra-inning games we had been leading and then let them slip away. In all my years in sports, I had never seen one game leave a team as devastated as we were following

Injury rehab with the Toledo Mud Hens.

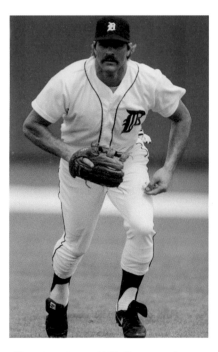

Charging in as Al Kaline taught me.

Saturday's crushing defeat. We trailed by 3½ games with seven left to play, and six remaining for the Jays.

Everyone writing or talking about baseball in Toronto that Saturday concluded that the East Division race was over. Most of the Tiger players were feeling the same way, as we tried to shake off the shock of losing three showdown games against a team we had planned to beat.

We lingered in front of our lockers at old Exhibition Stadium. At first we were thinking more than we were talking, sipping on a cold beer, no one in much of a hurry to move, as we waited for the last of the media to clear out. A group of us had gathered, including most of the key guys: Trammell, Whitaker, Lemon, Evans, Petry, Brookens, Grubb—pretty much the core of a team that had been united for so many years of struggle and glory.

We were talking seriously among ourselves. Deep into the discussion I blurted out, "Hey, boys, I think we just set the biggest bear trap of all time!" It came to me like a vision.

"They think it's over!" I said. My teammates looked at me like I was crazy, and they were certainly not following me. "We'll win this next game, get momentum on our side, and then ambush them like they've never seen before. They won't know what hit 'em."

The next day it almost was over, as a strong wind was blowing in from right field and we were down, 1–0, heading into the ninth against Toronto's fireballing closer, Tom Henke. It had been a frustrating day against the Blue Jays. We had hit several balls that would have been long gone anywhere else, but with the wind whipping in off Lake Ontario, our drives died and fluttered into routine flyouts. It seemed like the Mike Marshall batting cage episode all over again—no matter how hard the ball was hit that day, each time it was caught. The only thing missing was Coach Pellerin yelling, "Out!"

We were three outs from being closed out, all but mathematically eliminated—4½ games out with only 5 to play. I was leading off the ninth against Henke and decided that I would need to swing something lighter against the bullets he was throwing. I grabbed one of Bill Madlock's black bats, a little 32-ouncer that might help me get around on Henke's smoke.

He threw me a high fastball and I hit it a mile. That tied it, 1–1, and we were into a nail-biter that hung on until the 13th, when I got jammed on a tight pitch that broke my bat as I blooped a single that scored Jim Walewander. We won, 3–2, and the bear trap was set.

As the final week wore on, the Blue Jays struggled in a slow death as we sucked the life from them. George Bell, their big gun, was now begging for a hit, and by the time Toronto arrived in Detroit for the three-game weekend finale, the Jays had lost 3 games in a row. We were a single game out of first place.

We won Friday night, and beat them again on Saturday in 12 innings to take a one-game lead. Then on Sunday we got ready for what was going to be a dramatic regular-season finale. If the Jays won, we would meet again on Monday in a one-game playoff.

Veteran Frank Tanana put Toronto in knots, shutting the Jays out for nine innings, which enabled Larry Herndon—our quiet warrior—to be a hero. He hit an early home run, and we won, 1–0, to take the American League East Division title. Toronto had given us our chance by losing every one of their final seven games. We had believed in ourselves as a team, and together made a great comeback, learning to never give up. The trap had been sprung.

With all that we had shown during the second half of '87, we were favorites to clean up in the American League playoffs against Minnesota, which had won the West Division with a fairly anemic 85–77 record vs. our record of 98–64. We were more established and seemingly more talented, and had learned how to win in the post-season, while the Twins were young and not as impressive as some of our East Division competition.

We had an eighth-inning lead in Game One, but the Twins rallied to whip us, 8–5. It was the way things would go for Minnesota, who hammered us four games to one. They went on to beat St. Louis in seven games to take the World Series.

With the season over, I was off to my family and hunting the duck marshes, as I faced an off-season loaded with discussion

I CAN TELL YOU I DON'T LIKE TO SHAVE. I'M NOT GOING TO BE CLEAN-SHAVEN EVERY DAY. IT'S ALMOST PART OF MY MAKEUP, MY GAME. I FEEL NASTIER, I LIKE TO BE FIERCE, IT'S JUST PART OF MY UNIFORM. THAT SHOULD BE UNDERSTOOD.

A difference of opinion in the 1987 playoffs vs. Minnesota.

about Kirk Gibson's future in Detroit. I had played well enough for the Tigers in '87, but the front office was nervous about my upcoming free agency. It was only a year away. The Tigers were also aware that after another year in Detroit, I would have the authority to veto any trade to a team not of my liking, because of my status as a 10-season major-leaguer who had played at least five seasons with the same club.

In December, at baseball's Winter Meetings, Bill Lajoie actually agreed to a deal with Los Angeles that would have sent me to the Dodgers in exchange for Pedro Guerrero. But Dodgers insiders knew I was going to be declared an immediate free agent, so they backed out at the last minute.

The Dodgers' information had to do with a major grievance filed by the Players Association. It alleged that in 1985 several free agents—I was on that list—had been shut out of the market due to collusion on the part of baseball's owners. A decision was due from the arbitrator hearing the case, Tom Roberts, and the Dodgers felt I was going to be set free. This way they could sign me and still keep Guerrero.

And so I remained a Tiger until Roberts dropped the bomb that officially declared nine of us immediate free agents.

Then the Tigers began negotiating back and forth, but in our final talk, I told Bill Lajoie the posturing was over. "I'll take

$500,000 less to stay in Detroit." Lajoie called Tigers President Jim Campbell, who rejected the offer. I told Lajoie, "I respect your decision, even if I don't like it. Now please respect mine." On February 1, 1988, I signed a three-year, $4.5 million contract with the Los Angeles Dodgers. While the Tigers had been giving me all the reasons why I shouldn't be making that kind of money, the Dodgers had been telling me all the reasons why I should.

I flew to L.A. for an introductory press conference, and then JoAnn and I spent the next two weeks saying good-bye and packing for spring training at Vero Beach, Florida, as a member of the Los Angeles Dodgers.

In my natural element with Nick.

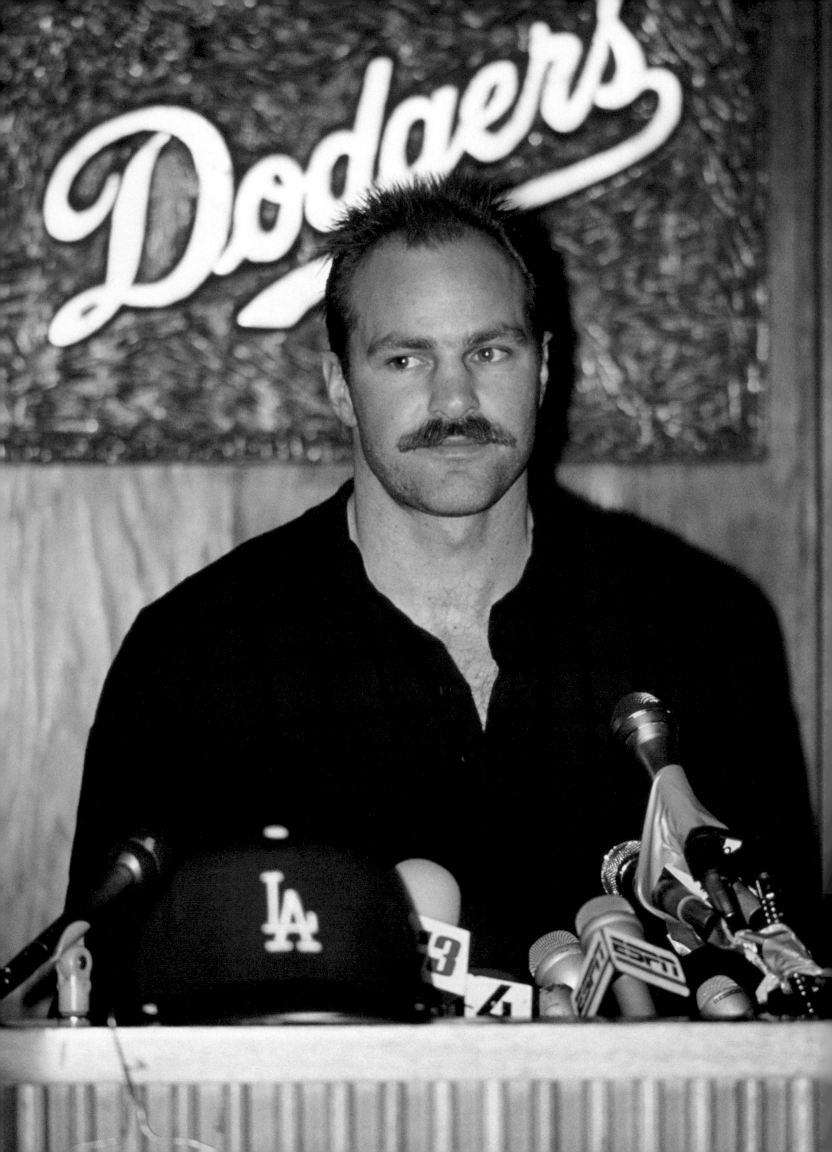

CHAPTER *nine*

"GIBSON...WAS A DISGRACE TO THE TIGER UNIFORM FOR HIS HALF-BEARD, HALF-STUBBLE," TOM MONAGHAN, THE TIGERS' OWNER, WROTE IN THE WEEKLY PUBLICATION THAT WENT TO EMPLOYEES OF HIS DOMINO'S PIZZA BUSINESS. "I DIDN'T LIKE HIS LONG HAIR."

A few days later, Monaghan was on the air with Detroit radio station WJR and told the late J.P. McCarthy that the Tigers would be much better off without me.

"His best talents, hitting home runs against right-handed pitchers, and stealing bases, are not worth a million and a half dollars a year," Monaghan said, "which means the best he could do for the Tigers would be as a DH against a right-handed pitcher. He has maybe one of the weaker arms in baseball for an outfielder, and can't field well. We don't need to replace Gibson."

What hurt me the most about Monaghan's comments was that nobody ever outworked or outprepared me—mentally or physically. I worked hard for the Tigers organization, and for my teammates. I picked my teammates up. I pushed them. I made them sacrifice. And now Monaghan was portraying me to the media and the fans as greedy and disloyal.

Detroit was my hometown. I had grown up there, and it hurt to read the letters to the editor the day of my departure for L.A. I thought the fans would understand why I had to make this decision for myself and my family.

What I thought of as being an obvious personal and family responsibility, they saw as ingratitude or opportunism. Columnists, commentators, letters to the editor, bar patron testimony on the 6 o'clock news—most of the old boosters now seemed to agree that Gibson had run out on them.

I just couldn't understand the criticism. After a rocky start, I had had a series of terrific years in Detroit, seasons in which I felt a return had been paid to the Detroit Tigers for their investment and their patience.

I loved playing baseball in Detroit. My home was here. My family and my wife's family all lived here. I boated on Lake St. Clair, my favorite duck marsh was nearby on the Canadian side of the lake, my buddies were in Michigan, and my real estate business was based near Detroit. My farm, my dogs, and my environment were all nearby as long as I played baseball for the Tigers.

But it still came down to a simple business deal in January of 1988 that could not be overlooked, and one I thought the Tigers were crazy not to understand, or to make adjustments toward. I was willing to take less—hundreds of thousands less—to stay in Detroit, but management wouldn't offer me a three-year contract. I wouldn't argue with the Tigers that I owed them for their support of me through injuries, disappointments, and scrapes, but I had given the Tigers the most dedicated, all-out competitive brand of baseball I could give. I had signed six one-year contracts, all along being told to be patient—even though they had signed other Tigers to long-term deals. The reward they kept alluding to never came. So it was off to another

Steve Sax and I sharing a laugh.

team that would be completely different, and a new challenge—Los Angeles.

The Dodgers were a sophisticated organization with a fabulous sense for making people feel good about themselves and, by extension, the ballclub. Everybody was sharp and upbeat. Better yet, there was personal warmth to match all the intelligence. I came to understand that was the way it all blended together under the owner, Peter O'Malley, who was taught by his father to run the team as a family business.

My wife, JoAnn, and I had a back-and-forth conversation about the move, and we were in complete harmony. We agreed: It's a three-year deal, it's Los Angeles, and it will be a good experience for us. We'll find out what life in Southern California is all about, enjoy a new organization, be exposed to new cultures, and make new friends. We decided to go for it.

When we reported to spring training in Vero Beach, Florida, it was incredible to see Los Angeles' fabulous complex, Dodgertown. It's a dream baseball facility, built on the concept that comfort and hospitality are central to a baseball club's success. Everything is perfect. There are conditioning facilities, a conference center, hotel, auditorium, perfect practice fields, and even a beautifully manicured golf course.

As for my new manager, Tommy Lasorda, it didn't take long for me to realize his style was different from Sparky Anderson's.

We would begin each day with a meeting that was on the playful side. Tommy would come in and immediately there would be some horseplay and someone would tell a joke, and then we'd get down to business. On our first day, Lasorda had the rookies and new guys stand up and introduce themselves, explaining who they were, where they had come from, and what they planned to accomplish with the Dodgers.

When they called my name, I stood up.

"My name is Kirk Gibson. I played football for Michigan State, I was a first-round draft pick by the Detroit Tigers, and I've been there my entire career. We won one world championship while I was in Detroit.

"I came to Los Angeles for one reason, and for one reason only, and that's to win a World Series trophy and ring. That is what's fun to me about baseball. I hate to lose. I *refuse* to lose. At times you may find me hard to live with as your teammate, but I think over time you'll realize that I'm one of the better teammates you'll have on this team, that I'll lay it all on the line for you, that I'll give you everything I've got. I'll fight for you. I'll be the best teammate you've ever had. Thank you very much.

"Oh yeah, one other thing. I have a wife and family and I value them more than anything."

I had not prepared this speech. It was the way I felt and it had an impact. Most of the guys just sat in front of their lockers, thinking, "Who's this?" I thought the winning theme had to be stressed. My first choice was to have stayed in Detroit. Now that I was in L.A., I was going to make the best of a new situation, even if I felt uncomfortable, a total outsider on a new team.

Warming up in Dodgertown.

In their approach to physical drills, the Dodgers were fairly serious. It was when we got to the playing field and began working on fundamentals that the atmosphere changed. Alarmingly, drills were loose. Way too loose for my tastes.

Soon after we began working on fielding bunts, Pedro Guerrero, who was playing third base, picked up a bunt and threw it into right field. Everybody began laughing at this silly throw that rocketed out of the infield.

I was stunned. These guys, this team, finished in fourth and fifth place the last two seasons, and it's funny to throw a ball into right field? This type of attitude made me burn inside. It was not how Kirk Gibson wanted to play baseball, even at spring training.

A couple of days later we were preparing to play our first spring game. It was my first game as a Dodger, bringing an extra edge to my preparations. I was totally juiced and had begun my pregame warm-ups in the outfield well ahead of everyone else. As the rest of the guys began arriving, I had already warmed up and started sweating. When I took my hat off to wipe the sweat from my head I saw everyone laughing, and sensed it was about me. I looked over at one of our bullpen coaches, Mark Cresse, who was standing nearby, and said tersely, "What's so funny?"

Making a diving catch in the outfield.

I'll never forget the look on his face. He knew immediately there was trouble. Nervously, he said, "I think somebody played a joke on you."

Someone had greased the inside of my cap with eye-black, and I had unknowingly wiped it all over myself. I was incensed.

I was standing near the left-field line and immediately broke into a three-quarter death jog, heading straight for the gate next to the visitors' clubhouse. I met Lasorda there and said, "Tommy, you find out what son of a bitch did this, because I'm going to tear his head off. I can't take this atmosphere any longer. You go find the SOB who did this!" And I ran off for the locker room.

Lasorda had no idea what had happened. He came in about 10 minutes later and said, "Oh, Kirk, they're just trying to make you part of the team. They were just trying to have some fun."

"Tommy," I said, "if they want to have fun, let's win some ballgames. Let's start picking up the ball and executing bunt plays, rundowns, running the bases properly, getting the fundamentals down. Without execution you can't win. You guys have finished fourth and fifth the last two years, and now I can see why. Now, you go find the son of a bitch who did it, and you bring him back, because I'm out of here in 10 minutes if I don't find out who it was. When I do find out, that's when I'll make a statement that this team will never forget. They're either with me or they're without me. If I don't fit in here, then you've got to get the owner and general manager together and get me out of here. To me, *winning* is what's fun."

Lasorda was trying hard to smooth it over. He could not believe I was making a big deal—a real scene, which would have repercussions—out of a practical joke.

He said, "Oh, Kirk, come on. You know the media's going to get this—"

"I don't care," I said to him. "We're going to get this thing out in the open. I'm going to make sure we're all on the same page."

I told him one more time that he had 10 minutes to deliver the joker to me, and that if I didn't find out who was responsible, I was out of there. He didn't make it back in time, and I left.

Obviously, Gibson had been in the lineup, then out of the lineup. Word traveled quickly that there had been an incident, and the media were looking for details.

I got a call at 6 a.m. the next morning. It was Lasorda.

"Kirk, how are you doing today?"

"I'm doing fine, Tommy. How are you?"

What has to be understood is that Lasorda and I at this point barely knew each other. There was no real sense for what the other person was all about. We were starting to find out.

"Yeah, Kirk, about the incident," he went on. "Could you stop by my room before you come in before practice? I'd like to talk with you."

"Yeah. I'll be right over."

I went over to Lasorda's room in Dodgertown, and Tommy very calmly sat down with me, speaking with perfect diplomacy.

"You know," he started off, "we've got a little problem here. I don't know about the place you came from, but the Dodgers really try and make sure that we are very positive with our press and..."

It was the customary stuff about the organization, and how it was a family—all the predictable Dodger Blue appeals.

"You've got to understand," he continued, "that they pulled a joke on you because they're just trying to make you feel comfortable. They play jokes..."

Lasorda went on for about 20 minutes. I never said a word. At the very end, he broke into a kind of Godfather mode.

"So here's what I'd like to do," he said. "I'd like to say that I excused you, that something personal came up, that it's all taken care of, and that you'll be in the lineup today."

"Mr. Lasorda," I said, "are you done?"

"Yeah."

"I understand everything you just said, and how you do everything here a bit differently. But I won't do what you just asked. I'm going to tell them the truth."

"Oh, Kirk, come on," Tommy moaned. He thought I was being stubborn.

"No," I said. "And let me tell you something else: I am very uncomfortable in this environment. I'm not saying I can change the whole thing, but we need to get serious here. Winning is fun. If you want to have fun, let's go out and kick people's butts. Let's get a World Series ring. We'll never have more fun than that. Sure, there are times to joke around. I don't have a problem with that. But once we hit the field, they've got to respect that I'm all business. There is no playing around.

"When you have your meeting today," I said to Tommy, "I want the guy who did it to come up and tell me he did it. Second, I want to stand up and talk to the team."

Lasorda knew from my tone and my persistence that I had to stand up and talk to the team. He finally agreed.

I went back into a very tense clubhouse that was normally loose and jovial. No one would even look at me. They all knew what had happened. My feelings had not changed. A statement needed to be made.

I stepped out of the locker room, and in a few moments I was approached rather timidly by one of our pitchers, Jesse Orosco.

His hands were shaking when he greeted me.

"Hi, buddy," he stammered.

Knowing how angry I was at him, I just wanted him out of my way, so I wouldn't be tempted to go after him. I just looked at him with contempt and said, "You don't know me. Get out of my face."

A few minutes later, inside the clubhouse, Lasorda convened his morning meeting. The atmosphere was stone cold silence, and the players could feel my intensity radiating. Lasorda announced, "Kirk would like to say something."

I wasn't sure how it would be received, and I didn't really care. I stood up and explained to everyone the brand of competitiveness I believed in.

"On a bunt play you guys throw balls into right field," I said. "You laugh, even though we've got to execute it correctly in a game. I've watched you guys on TV. Blowing plays like that is why, when you play St. Louis, they just keep running the bases.

Showing the intensity that rubbed off on the Dodgers in 1988.

"What are we here for? We're here to be world champions. You know what? I've been a world champion. You don't become world champions by just stumbling into it.

"We're getting ready to enter the marathon race," I went on. "We're going to see how much heart we have. If we haven't got heart, we haven't got a prayer. We've got to start challenging ourselves mentally—now, because it's going to get a lot worse than this.

"If I'm wrong, then I'm on the wrong team, the front office will move me, and you guys can go your own route. Now if anybody's got a problem with what I've said...TOUGH. I'm standing right here. If you want me—one of you, all of you—I don't care. I will do anything to prove to you that I'm here to sacrifice in order to become world champions."

Though I may have overreacted, I said some things that were true, and that needed to be said. The tone of our team was different from that day on.

Part of my need to talk so heatedly to the players is that I had been through the good and the bad. I was 30 years old. I had seen how a lack of focus could hurt a team. I had gone through a dramatic turnaround that changed my entire approach to baseball, and to my life. That rededication had enabled me, and the Detroit Tigers, to play at maximum capability. The end result was a World Series ring.

I had been so scalded by the early failures, and so inspired by the results from a changeover, that I could no longer tolerate anything less than total dedication to excellence. There was a time for having fun. It was a clearly defined time, and I had my share of it, but that time did not infringe on preparing for a game, or on something as serious as practice drills.

I could see we had our share of gamers: Steve Sax, Mike Marshall, Mickey Hatcher, John Shelby, Orel Hershiser. I just wasn't so sure if, in too many other cases, there might not be something to this Southern California stereotype of laid-back beach guys approaching every day leisurely, rather than as a responsibility. We would find out.

Another big change for me that season was my approach to hitting, thanks to our hitting coach, Ben Hines. For the first time in my life I broke down the mechanics of the swing and considered the way they affected a thrown baseball. I thought about how I could use the entire field, as opposed to my usual habit of pulling everything to right field.

Every day I worked with Ben, focusing on ways to keep my hands inside. I learned how to shorten the arc of my swing. He taught me to hit a baseball with backspin, or sidespin. Backspin would create more lift and turn some of those hard shots into home runs and extra-base gappers into the power alleys. Sidespin was the product of a good hitting habit—keeping my hands inside, rather than coming over the top on the ball. I could then stay behind the ball to a greater degree, waiting on it, and, depending upon location, hit it hard to the opposite field. Defending me would then be much tougher.

My personal development had kicked into gear, much the way our entire team seemed to be taking on depth and dimension. As slowly as we started, adjusting to each other with all the new faces, we left Florida in good shape and, in our minds, we were a good bet to shake up the National League West, though most experts picked us to finish no better than middle-of-the-pack.

Two Dodger MVPs, Orel Hershiser and Kirk Gibson.

Best of all, I now felt I was part of a team. My intensity became their intensity. On the field, I was vicious, and it was rubbing off on my teammates.

We got off to a good start, and on May 26, surprising the baseball experts, we moved into first place, which is where we would stick for the remainder of the season. I hit .323 in May and stayed in a groove the rest of the way. More important, I watched this team really begin to appreciate what happens when you play opposing teams tough. Even when we were losing, we wouldn't give up until the last out.

You wear the other teams down—both physically and mentally—so that they come to hate playing you. It was part of my football mindset on display at Dodger Stadium—the "mental" press. I'm not sure everyone had viewed the Dodgers in quite that light during the '80s, but we were becoming a dangerous, nasty, relentless National League team, and I was loving it.

In August, we were putting together a seven-game winning streak that pushed our lead to 5½ games. We were aggressive. We were pressing opposing teams. During that streak, in a game against Montreal at Dodger Stadium, we were trailing, 3–2, heading into the bottom of the ninth. I singled home the tying run off Joe Hesketh. Then I stole second base. While on second, I was calculating my chances of going for home on a wild pitch or a passed ball. Surprise would be my advantage. Hesketh threw a lot of balls that got by the catcher, and he had broken his leg trying to cover home plate before. There was also a long way between home plate and the backstop at Dodger Stadium, so it would take the catcher longer to retrieve the ball if it got past him. Calculating all that, I was ready to run full speed—not even thinking of stopping at third—all the way home, at the first hint that a Hesketh pitch was getting by the catcher. When his next pitch skidded by, I was off. If Hesketh was going to try to stop me at the plate, he was going to pay for it.

As I steamed around third, I liked my chances in what 10 years earlier would have been a gallop for the end zone. I practically left an excavation at the point where I began my slide, and skidded across home plate, beating the tag, as we won, 4–3.

Scratch-and-claw battles like this are what gives teams an edge, and now we had that edge.

Juan Samuel goes high to avoid my slide into second.

"HE HAS REALLY BEEN THE HEART AND SOUL OF THIS BALLCLUB. HE MADE IT RIGHT AND HE MADE IT COOL TO WORK HARD AND BE A HUSTLER. HIS HARD WORK GAVE HIM THE RIGHT TO TALK TO PEOPLE AND AIR THEM OUT AND MAKE THEM PROUD TO BE DODGERS."

—*Orel Hershiser*

Tommy Lasorda had a different approach, certainly, from Sparky Anderson when it came to running his ballclub. To me, the differences were simple variations in personality. When you got right down to it, there was no *real* difference. Each man was a fierce, fierce competitor, so the distinctions in personal makeup were irrelevant.

Tommy, though, had one habit that made him a different skipper altogether. He threw batting practice. The old Dodgers left-hander could not forget his heritage, so he was always out there, throwing me one breaking pitch after another. We ragged him about it mercilessly.

"Tommy, move up," we would yell, pounding him for not throwing harder. As if a 60-year-old man was going to throw smoke. We didn't care what he threw. It was the razzing we delighted in, and it really heated up during spring training.

"No!" he'd snap back at us. "I am not moving up. The day I've got to move up, I quit!"

Lasorda had a colorful reputation as the funny man who liked to eat. It was absolutely true. You would go into his office and there would be food every-where: cheese, seafood, pasta, Mexican food—you name it.

Often, we would fly into a particular town at the start of a road trip, have the evening free, and as we got to the hotel,

Tommy would say, "Okay, everybody down in the lobby in 20 minutes." We would meet and he would take all of us to a restaurant for a big dinner together. To Tommy, these sessions weren't meetings, they were "eatings," and it was a great way to relax and have some fun with teammates.

We continued our tenacious play through summer, a world away from all the clowning that had taken place in spring training.

Every player on the team had a role to play, and each man came through when the team needed it. Alfredo Griffin was a good example. A dynamite shortstop, Griff was barely hitting .200, but if the bases were loaded, you could count on him driving everyone home. When he went down with a broken hand, Dave Anderson moved in, and did an awesome job. At catcher we had Mike Scioscia, who blocked runners at the plate better than anyone in baseball. We were wearing the other teams down, and by September 26 we had clinched the National League West Division title. Still, we were underdogs heading into the National League Championship playoffs against the mighty New York Mets. The Mets were loaded with talent, led by Dwight Gooden and Daryl Strawberry, both at the height of their careers.

I went into the playoffs with a host of injuries that had plagued me since the midway point of my 1988 season. Sometimes the origin of a hamstring problem might blend in with a dozen other hurts, so that after a while you didn't really think about exactly where the pain was coming from.

Struggling early in the National League Championship against the Mets.

125

A home run in the wee hours against New York that turned the momentum.

But it hadn't slowed me down. I scored 106 runs that season, and never ran the bases better, or harder. I might get three hits, maybe leg out a triple or take out a second baseman to break up a double play, but I went full tilt, all game, every day, all season.

The Mets jumped out to win two of the first three games in our best-of-seven showdown. There was only one thought in our minds preparing for Game Four. It would be virtually impossible to come back against the Mets if we found ourselves down three games to one. I had contributed nothing. I had gone 1 for 16 through the first three games, and looked lousy doing it. Now we were in the ninth inning of Game Four at Shea Stadium, down 4–2, just three outs away from being in that very hole. Worse, Dwight Gooden was in Cy Young form. Fortunately, Mike Scioscia finally caught up with one of Gooden's fastballs and knocked it into the seats—a two-run shot in the ninth—to tie the game 4–4 and send it into an overtime thriller. Then, in the 12th, in a game that was now approaching 1 a.m. in New York, I came to life and clubbed one deep into the right-center bleachers off Roger McDowell, as we won 5–4 and evened the series at two games apiece. It was a huge turnaround for us. We had learned during the season the advantages of not giving up, and that home run gave everyone the sense—including the Mets—that we could win the National League Championship.

I was so pumped up, my adrenaline surging with playoff tension and excitement. The game ended after 1 a.m., and after talking to the media, showering, and getting back to the hotel, it was almost 4 a.m. by the time I got to my room. I just lay in bed, unable to sleep. Finally I got up to pack for the trip back to L.A. after Game Five. My mind was reeling with thoughts of wanting to play our noon game right now. After fending off certain defeat, I *knew* we could win the next game.

Only half a day after the early morning dramatics in Game Four, I hit a three-run bomb off Sid Fernandez into Shea Stadium's upper deck to reinforce our confidence, as we won, 7–4, to take a 3–2 series lead. Unfortunately, in the ninth inning, feeling we needed an insurance run, I stole second base and

All eyes are watching this 3-run shot in Game 5.

The first of my two major leg injuries in the NL Championship.

YEAH, THERE ARE SOME THINGS I HAVE TO DO. I'M GOING TO ABUSE MY BODY AND THE BASTARD DOWN THERE TRYING TO TURN THE DOUBLE PLAY WHEN THAT'S WHAT IT TAKES. HELL, IT FEELS GOOD TO HURT WHEN YOU'RE WINNING.

felt a pop behind my left knee. It knotted up, and I knew it was bad. I called time and hobbled off the field to a standing ovation. That's the way it could be in a hostile stadium, and certainly Shea was that. The New York fans cheered my departure.

An injection of cortisone from the doctors got me through Game Six, a 5–1 defeat. In Game Seven, another problem arose. Trying to protect my bad leg, I made an ugly slide as I attempted to break up a double play. In doing so I strained the medial collateral ligament in my other knee. Both legs were now shot. The good news was that we won Game Seven, 6–0. We now had to face the dominant and powerful American League Champion Oakland A's, led by the "Bash Brothers"— Jose Canseco and Mark McGwire.

The trainers and doctors worked nonstop, looking at the problems in both legs, and giving me injections they hoped might mask the excruciating pain from disabling injuries that would only heal with extended off-season rest.

The doctors sent me home to elevate my legs. They had done all they could, hoping for some miracle that I would wake up and be ready to play. When I woke up the next morning I walked lightly, and I thought maybe a miracle *had* happened. But when I tried to jog, my legs were nearly ready to collapse from the pain. I realized this was a level of pain I'd never had to perform with before. I was afraid I wouldn't be able to play in the type of game I lived for, where the World Championship was at stake.

I got to Dodger Stadium early and leveled with Tommy Lasorda: "Tommy, this is bad. I'm really hurt. I don't know if I can do it tonight."

Dr. Frank Jobe—one of the world leaders in sports medicine—and his staff came into the office, sized up the situation, and we unanimously agreed that I was out.

I told Tommy and the team, the best I could, how I felt. But words were awfully thin in this circumstance, which was as depressing as any moment I had known. To have worked so hard for an entire season, to have been someone the guys relied on each day for 162 games—to be in the World Series and not play.

"I'm crushed," I told them. "I want to be out there, and I can't even go out for introductions." I sat in the clubhouse as the teams were introduced, and as the crowd roared, the World Series began taking place—all without me.

I was reduced to sitting in the clubhouse, watching the World Series on television, no different from any average fan. All I could do was put ice packs on two tormentingly painful legs that were keeping me out of the biggest baseball game in the world. The mental agony was as bad as the physical.

Reluctantly leaving the field following my injury.

Overwhelmed with a sense of helplessness before Game 1 in the World Series.

I heard NBC's Vin Scully say, over and over, "Gibson will not be playing tonight. He's not even in the dugout." Something about the finality of his words agitated me, made me angry. My mind began rumbling. I was beginning to feel energy from the game. I began to visualize scenes and moments. I visualized one final at-bat. I knew that Oakland's right-handed relief ace, Dennis Eckersley, the dominant closer in baseball that year, would be on the mound in the ninth inning to finish the Dodgers off. Now I was visualizing winning the game. One shot. One at-bat. It was all I could give, my only chance to contribute.

Jose Canseco had ripped an early grand slam home run—a shot so hard it nearly hit a cameraman in deep centerfield—and Oakland was still leading by a run, 4–3, as the eighth inning came to a close. We were running out of players, and Eckersley was coming in to finish us off.

Scully said, "Looking to the ninth for the Dodgers, it will be Mike Scioscia, Jeff Hamilton, and Alfredo Griffin, followed by the pitcher. All the Dodgers have remaining on the bench are Dave Anderson, Mike Davis, and Kirk Gibson, but we know he's not going to be playing."

"My ass," I said.

I began visualizing the crowd, thinking of their response when I walked out of the dugout. I thought, "When I hear 55,000 loyal Dodger fans going nuts, I won't hurt anymore." Now I had the image, as big as a movie screen, vividly developed in my mind. I was going to sting Eckersley and win the game.

I peeled off the ice bags, dropping them on the floor, and walked straight to my locker. I grabbed Mitch Poole, our clubhouse attendant, and told him to get the batting tee and set it up in the hitting net that was located at the top of a runway that led down to the dugout.

"What?"

"Set it up," I said. "Hurry!"

I put on just enough of a uniform to be legal, then grabbed my batting glove and a bat, and headed over to the net. Mitch was there, placing baseballs on the tee as I took some cuts. I was hitting—and hurting. My legs were frozen from all the ice.

"Go get Tommy," I told Mitch, who still couldn't believe what he was seeing.

"GO GET TOMMY!"

I heard him run down the ramp to the dugout and, of course, Tommy was all stressed out, as Game One was being shut tight with Eckersley pitching. Lasorda saw Mitch and growled, "Goddammit, I've got a game going on here."

"It's Gibby—he wants you."

Tommy came waddling up the tunnel, and I will never forget the sight. He looked as if he had seen a ghost.

I said, "Hit Davis eighth. I'll hit for the pitcher."

Lasorda turned around and headed hell-bent for the dugout. He was shaking his head, and all I heard was his murmuring as he disappeared down the tunnel—"Holy Christ." Then he yelled back, "You stay up there until I come and get you!"

Tommy might have been excited, but he wasn't forgetting his strategy. If the Athletics didn't see me in the dugout, they would likely pitch more carefully to Davis, who had enough power to hit a home run to tie the game, than light-hitting Dave Anderson, who would be standing in the on-deck circle.

Eckersley stuck to the script, getting Mike Scioscia on a pop-up, then striking out Jeff Hamilton. We were one out away from losing the opening game—and the huge momentum we had built up in our series against the Mets. Lasorda went along with the plan, opting to pinch-hit the left-hand-hitting Davis for Alfredo Griffin. Davis worked the count to 2–1, then 3–1. I couldn't stand it any longer. I began creeping toward the dugout. Ball four.

I had stepped into the dugout and was now climbing up the steps and onto the field. As I hoisted myself up the steps and into view, Dodger Stadium erupted. The place rocked, and the sounds were numbing. I shuffled to the on-deck circle, grabbed a rosin bag, threw it down, and walked straight for the plate. Just as I had anticipated, the pain became secondary to the deafening roar of the crowd.

Eckersley, who thought he owned all hitters, was ready for me. He had not watched as I gimped over to the plate. I stared out, looked him in the eye, and said to myself, "Bring it on. I got you. This is what I've been waiting for."

You could see in Eckersley's face that he was ready to set me down to end the game. I was locked on to my imagery. It was time.

Eckersley's first pitch was a fastball that I fouled off to the left. I hadn't come close to getting around on it, and I limped as I swung. He came hard with another fastball and I fouled this one off as well, back into the loge seats. A better cut, but I was still just flicking the bat at his fastball. Now it was 0 and 2. I must have looked helpless, and the game was looking that way as well, but it wasn't what I was visualizing. I went into my emergency mode, protecting the plate, guarding against a strikeout. He threw another fastball that I was lucky to dribble foul down the first-base line. Between pitches I was pounding the bat against my cleats harder and harder with each pitch. I dug in for another 0 and 2 pitch. Ball one, outside.

Eckersley got set for his fifth pitch, the crowd hysterical from tension. Again, I was lucky to foul off another fastball. Still 1 and 2.

Eckersley came back with another fastball that was high and outside. The count went to 2 and 2. When Eckersley would throw back to first to check Davis, the loyal Dodger crowd gave a long chorus of boos. This at-bat was turning into a classic battle of the minds—Eckersley vs. Gibson. The mental pressure was what I liked. It made me better. I was focused. I had affirmed and visualized exactly what I needed to do.

Eckersley went the other way, this time with an inside breaking ball, which I took. Davis was running on the pitch and made it into second easily. The count was now 3 and 2. As Eckersley started his motion, I called time.

I stepped out of the box as the words of our advance scout, Mel Didier—the same Mel Didier who had tried to persuade

Seattle to draft me 10 years earlier—rang in my mind as clearly as if he were standing next to me.

Dennis Eckersley's 3-2 backdoor slider: Image x Vividness = Reality.

"Paarrrtner," he drawled, speaking to me before the Series began, "as sure as I'm standing here breathin', if Eckersley goes 3 and 2 on you, you're goin' to see a backdoor slider. I've seen him freeze George Brett with it. I've seen him freeze Wade Boggs. If you get him to 3 and 2, get ready to step into it, because it will be that backdoor slider." As I got back into the batter's box the crowd roared with anticipation.

Eckersley got set, and here it came, just as promised—the backdoor slider. I stepped into it, and I'm not sure a human being alive has experienced the feeling that flooded my mind and body as the ball rocketed into the darkness. At the moment it jumped off my bat I knew it was gone. I watched it arc into the right-field seats, and heard the stadium explode into shrieks, understanding in an instant all that this home run meant, as the crowd shook Dodger Stadium and people in front of TV sets all across the country cheered in delight.

I must have been quite a sight, limping around the bases. I was moving, but barely.

What I couldn't make my legs do, I let my right arm accomplish. I pumped the arm, hard, celebrating a triumph over every damned foe I had battled over the last 10 years.

133

I discovered later that the at-bat lasted more than seven minutes. NBC went silent for a minute and eight seconds after the home run was hit. The crowd celebrated so hard, they rocked Dodger Stadium to the point that the TV cameras shook.

The home run turned the momentum to our side. We now knew we *could* win. It was my only at-bat in the series, but it helped lead us to a World Series Championship in five games.

From smearing eye-black in a guy's cap to a World Series ring. It was a yearlong classroom. Commitment. Dedication. Teamwork. Championship Ring.

A run of a lifetime.

CHAPTER *ten*

I HAD BEEN NAMED NATIONAL LEAGUE MOST VALUABLE

PLAYER. THERE HAD BEEN THE BIG HOME RUN AND THE SATIS-

FACTION OF KNOWING I HAD PLAYED HARD AND HELPED TO MAKE

A DIFFERENCE ON A CLUB THAT WAS LOADED WITH CONTRIBUTORS AND

HAD AN OLD-FASHIONED BASEBALL ETHIC.

I even got a phone call from Tom Monaghan, the Detroit Tigers owner who one year earlier had said I was a disgrace to the club. He had left a message with my business associate. When I called Monaghan back, he was pleasant and conciliatory.

"I just wanted to apologize," he said, and he went on at length in an effort to make amends for the things he had said and written after I signed with L.A. He also wanted me to stop by his Domino's Pizza headquarters—Domino Farms—and have lunch with him.

I was polite but direct.

"Mr. Monaghan, you're a year late with your phone call," I began. "I question your motivation for calling me. We have nothing in common. We have no reason to have lunch together. From the little bit that I know you, I would say that you're trying to put together a little public relations event here, where I come in and have lunch, and you have them snap a few shots of us, smiling, and then everything's fine. But it's not. It won't be. Good luck with your team. Good-bye."

I felt it was a necessary response. I had never gone public with my feelings toward him or toward the words he had used a year earlier. I had determined that my on-field actions would be my public retort against people who doubted me. More important, my performance would vindicate those who had never lost faith in me. Now, as one of my main doubters, Monaghan needed to be told that personal insults of the kind delivered against me and—to my mind—against my family, were not about to be smoothed over by some happy-talk P.R. luncheon.

Our discussion at least provided some resolution as I prepared for a 1989 season with a club that, by contrast, seemed always to be inventing ways to make a player feel good about playing for them. Considering everything that had happened throughout our 1988 dream, I suppose things were destined to go less than perfectly in '89.

In fact, the follow-up was a disaster.

The same hamstring problem that had shelved me in the World Series was flaring up again. I had rested and rehabbed it throughout the off-season, but it was by no means 100 percent when I got to camp. Lasorda asked me right away how it felt.

"It's not right," I said. "It's not healed, whatever it is. But if you want me in there, I'll be there for you."

He said, "I want you in the lineup."

1988 World Series celebration.

So I played. And it hurt. And it would not cease hurting.

The Dodgers medical staff did test after test and could find nothing wrong. By midseason, I could no longer stand it. I got a second opinion. Still, nothing conclusive. The Dodgers staff agreed that we would try one more time to rehab the leg, and if there were still no progress, we would go ahead with exploratory surgery.

In the Dodgers clubhouse was a speedbag that I used as part of my conditioning program. I worked on it hard one night, and the next morning I could barely walk. I decided at that moment that we had hit a wall. I wanted to schedule surgery.

To make a long medical discussion short, they opened up my leg, saw nothing obvious, then decided to invade the sheath surrounding my hamstring tendon. The moment they cut into it, a mess of tissue and debris burst from the sheath.

There, at long last, was the answer. Fully fifty percent of my hamstring had torn, had frayed like strands of a cable. Dead, degenerative tissue had knotted up and bulged, sliding up and down within the sheath each time I took a step. Small wonder the thing had been killing me.

The doctors cleaned up the tendon, sewed me up, and

probably resisted an urge to shake me awake to announce the good news. But I was still a long way from home. As any athlete who has had such problems knows, recovering from a bad hamstring is a long, long process. In my case, it would be 1992, three years later, before it totally healed.

My initial rehabilitation from surgery lasted nearly 10 months. The Dodgers did not reactivate me until June 2, 1990. In some respects, the rest may have been a blessing, since I was also recovering from an experience that had nearly cost me my life.

Following a game in late spring of 1989, my family and I were returning to our home in Santa Monica and decided to stop for dinner at a restaurant, Apple's, on Wilshire Boulevard. JoAnn, who was pregnant with our second child, Kevin, had driven to the game separately, bringing along our oldest son, Kirk Robert, who was a few months shy of 3, and Colleen, JoAnn's daughter from her first marriage.

We were driving along 25th Street en route to the house, with my car in the lead, when JoAnn noticed that a vehicle seemed to be following. I was unaware of a third party. We stayed on the road and made our way into the driveway of our home. I hit the garage-door opener and pulled into the garage and opened the door to remove Kirk Robert from his rear carseat.

JoAnn and Colleen pulled in the driveway, at which point JoAnn got out of the car and began walking toward me. She thought I should know that something seemed fishy about the car that had been shadowing us.

And then I saw him. A guy was running up the driveway with a handgun aimed straight at me. He jammed the barrel into my chest. I put up my hands, desperate to keep this kid, who was probably 19 or 20, from pulling the trigger. JoAnn and the kids were distraught.

"Hey, man, just be cool," I said. "I don't know what you're after. We obviously don't want any trouble here. Stay calm. Let's talk it out. I'll give you what you want."

On my face and across my head I could feel the chill from my sweat. The terror was, and remains to this day, indescribable. I was absorbed by a single thought: to remain calm. Yet anyone who has been involved in this kind of horror understands, instinctively, that nervousness or agitation can get an entire family killed.

I told JoAnn and the kids to move out of the driveway and to the other side of the car. I wanted them as far away from the danger as possible.

"Get in the car," he said, and as I climbed carefully into the driver's seat, he stood outside the car and held the pistol flush against my temple.

MY GOAL COMING OUT OF SPRING TRAINING WAS TO BE THE WORLD CHAMPIONS, THAT'S ALL. IT'S ALL I THOUGHT ABOUT. NOT THE ALL-STAR GAME OR WINNING THE MVP. NOTHING ELSE MADE A DIFFERENCE TO ME.

Another impromptu sprint with Kirk Robert, carrying on my father's tradition.

It was a 9-mm Beretta. I owned one identical to it. I could see an exposed red dot at the rear of the cylinder, which meant the safety was in an "off" position. The slightest bit of pressure on the trigger and I was dead.

"Start the car," he said.

I started the car, a 750 BMW, and as it began to idle, he ordered me out of the car.

"I know you carry lots of money," he said. "Give me your money."

I carefully removed all of the cash from my pocket, $800, and handed it to him. He grabbed it, jumped into the car, backed out of the driveway and tore off. I'm not sure at what point his accomplice, or accomplices, had left in the car that followed JoAnn. But they were all gone now.

That's when the piercing screams from JoAnn and the kids began, exceeding anything that movie sets or Hollywood stars could duplicate. It was terror unleashed. We had come within a wrong move, even a facial expression—of having our family shattered.

I called 911, trying to act and speak clear-headedly. It seemed as if any degree of calm would help against all the emotional trauma. The police came and we spent a long time filing reports and going over the incident. It was an ambush car-jacking all the way. The BMW was eventually recovered, stripped to the core. But no one was ever charged or prosecuted.

I did not sleep for two consecutive nights following the holdup. I did not close my eyes, because of the terror, the anger—the total inability to get past an experience that had nearly produced tragedy. I sent JoAnn and the kids back to Detroit and checked into a hotel. And that's where I lived for the remainder of the season, until my August surgery.

The following year we moved into a high-rise in Glendale that had 24-hour security. We were not—within our control, anyway—going to allow anything approaching the Santa Monica experience to happen again.

But the damage was permanent. I wanted away from something that had created such upset for me and my family. I wanted to go home and to get away from L.A. It wasn't the community's fault, but it was natural to want to distance ourselves from an incident so searing.

The Dodgers accepted my feelings, and were reasonable when I asked them in 1990 if a trade to an American League club, closer to Detroit, might be possible. It didn't happen. My hamstring made me a part-timer during the '89 and '90 seasons, and I'm not sure there would have been great inclination on L.A.'s part to sign me beyond our three-year deal, even if my feelings had been different. I had given the club a boost during the course of one glorious year, all before a bad leg and a terrible incident conspired to ruin the following two seasons.

And so I got ready to try to get a career back on track in a new town. The only problem was, I had no idea where.

CHAPTER *eleven*

I WANTED TO GO HOME AND TO PLAY AGAIN IN DETROIT. I

WANTED BADLY TO BE REUNITED WITH ALL THE PEOPLE—FAMILY,

FRIENDS, AND TIGER TEAMMATES—WHO HAD INFLUENCED MY

LIFE, BOTH PERSONALLY AND AS A MAJOR LEAGUE BASEBALL PLAYER.

The only hang-up, as a lousy 1990 season closed and I prepared to leave Los Angeles, was that the Detroit Tigers wanted no part of me. That had been the decree of Tigers president Jim Campbell, when I signed with the Dodgers in February of 1988. Campbell believed I had deserted a loyal employer, and that because of my decision I was to be forever banished from Detroit. He had said it privately to those within the club. "Kirk Gibson will never again wear a Detroit uniform."

At a time when I would have been a reasonable buy for a Detroit club that certainly needed help, I was out of luck, and had to search elsewhere for a home.

Kansas City headed a short list. It was an easy choice. Playing there would mean a return to a simpler Midwestern life that looked especially inviting after the busy pace in L.A.

I signed a two-year contract for $3 million and prepared to become a full-time designated hitter for a team that had a lot of promise—until injuries began wrecking us. Bo Jackson was lost to a hip injury. Hall of Famer George Brett went out with a bad knee. Power hitter Danny Tartabull got hurt. Third baseman Kevin Seitzer got hurt. Suddenly half our lineup was gone, and I ended up as the everyday left fielder—on artificial turf, which puts much more stress on your body than natural grass.

I hit six home runs in April and had a good start, but my season seemed to go the way of the club's. We weren't healthy, and we struggled. Our manager, John Wathan, a man I had played against and a person I liked, was fired at mid-season and replaced by Hal McRae. That pretty much ended it for me in Kansas City.

McRae laughs it off today, but there had been problems between us stemming from my rookie year back in Detroit. Prior to a game that season, I was taking early batting practice, and McRae, who was playing for K.C. at that time, and who was a real talker, was getting all over me about my college football days. It was "football player" this and "football player" that, and, "Let's see how hard a football player is supposed to hit," and I had no patience for any rookie baiting.

I walked out of the cage, got down into a three-point stance, and said hotly, "Don't talk that stuff on me. Why don't you just see how hard this football player can hit, or shut up! Now, what's it going to be?"

I doubt that he ever forgot that challenge, and I believe the friction was still there 12 years later. In 1991 I had only hit .236 with 16 home runs and 55 RBIs on a last place team. Although I had been signed as a DH, I played left field every game hard on a post-rehab leg. In the

Signed to DH in Kansas City, I ended up as an everyday outfielder.

The key players in my Kansas City stay.

off-season, I worked hard to make an improvement on the previous year, and knew I would come into camp in '92 with a shot at helping K.C. win a division title.

Instead, I got to the Royals spring training camp in Haines City, Florida, and McRae informed me that I "would not be given an opportunity to win an everyday job." I said to him, "Look, I'm here to tell you that I wasn't happy with the way I played last year either. But I've been getting up at 6 o'clock in the morning and working out to erase those bad memories. Now, I'm walking into spring training and you're going to tell me I have no chance to compete for a job?"

McRae said, "That's exactly what I'm telling you."

I was on fire.

"Well, you just better get me out of here, because I won't suck that up," I said. "I won't have somebody telling me that I'm here to go through the motions. I won't have somebody down here telling me that I'm not going to have an opportunity to make this a world championship club."

Two or three weeks had passed when we met in the office of Herk Robinson, the Royals general manager. My temperament had not changed. McRae explained his position of wanting

younger players, then gave me a little smile to rub it in. Twelve years earlier I would have gone after him.

I told him, "Wipe that smile off your face right now, because I'm serious! There's nothing funny about this at all. I'll only respect the fact that you're the manager so far. You and I appear to have conflicting personalities, and I think it's good for everybody—unless you're going to give me an opportunity to compete—to move me."

On March 10, after a fair amount of public popping off on my part, I was traded to Pittsburgh for a left-handed pitcher, Neal Heaton. The Pirates would not have been my first choice, but it was reasonably close to Detroit and provided me with a chance to play regularly and to help a club that was managed by my old minor league professor, Jim Leyland.

I got off to a slow start through the first month of the regular season. I was hitting below the "Mendoza" line—only .196—but in my mind things were coming around, when Leyland called me into his office on May 12.

He was, typically, up-front. He said the Pirates were releasing me, that it was his decision, and that he wished me the best of luck.

"Fine," I said. We shook hands, I grabbed my car, went back to the Pittsburgh hotel where I was living, packed my things, and was on the road home. I had cleared waivers, which meant no other team wanted me. I was retired from baseball, whether I wanted to be or not.

I didn't know what to think. It was rough on the psyche, being told at age 34 that I no longer had it, when I felt quite the opposite. As I drove home to Detroit on the Ohio Turnpike, I was partly in shock and partly relieved. Since 1988, nothing had seemed to work out right. In fact, it had been downright mentally draining—maybe it *was* time to retire. I called my mom to tell her the news, and that really gave it a sense of finality.

It was nice to think about being home with JoAnn and the kids. I liked the idea of having a summer free with the family. I looked forward to making some necessary changes that would reshape the way I managed my business and my real estate ventures.

It was difficult for me to understand front-office attitudes that suggested I could no longer benefit a major-league team. I genuinely believed that I still had a lot of games in me. But one of the more enjoyable summers of my life began to unfold at home with my wife and sons. It was a new and exciting experience for me because, as a professional athlete, you don't get to spend enough time with your family.

It would have remained that way had Tom Monaghan not sold the Detroit Tigers to Mike Ilitch, head of the Little Caesar's pizza empire. Ilitch was a progressive businessman who had invested heavily in resurrecting the Detroit Red Wings and making them a Stanley Cup contender.

He had a similar plan for the Tigers, although Ilitch would discover that building a winning club in baseball can be more expensive and uncertain than anything he had faced in the NHL. A key in Ilitch's sports and business dealings was Gary Vitto, an assistant general manager with the Tigers.

Vitto helped persuade Ilitch that I should be playing for the Tigers, an effort that began gaining steam during the winter of 1992–93.

During lunch one day at a downtown restaurant, a friend of mine had overheard Ilitch say, "I've got to have Kirk Gibson on this team. I love the intensity that he plays with."

Ilitch was the boss, without question, but he respected the expertise of his front-office people. Jim Campbell had retired and been replaced by general manager, Jerry Walker. Walker wasn't overly interested in bringing aboard a 35-year-old player who nearly a year earlier had washed out of baseball. At Ilitch's urging, Walker called to talk it over some more. After some introductory discussion, I invited him to my house.

When Walker arrived, he showed very little enthusiasm. I kept looking at him as we talked, noticing how he would glance away when he spoke—never looking me in the eye. He was saying all the right things—that I could be a plus on the club—

but his body language made it clear that he was skeptical that I could still play and contribute. He left, making no commitment.

This stalling got to such a point of frustration that I finally drove to Tiger Stadium for one final meeting with Walker.

"Jerry, do you want me on this team?" I asked. "Do you really want me on this team? I don't want you playing games with me."

Across his face there flashed this sincere, almost remorseful expression. He said, "Yeah, I think you'd be great for our team. I don't know how much money we have, and we might have to take someone else off the roster."

"Fine," I said, now feeling that one way or the other it would be resolved. "Go get a blank contract—I'll sign it, and you fill in the numbers."

And that's how we got it done. It was a fairly safe investment for the Tigers: a one-year contract for $500,000, with incentives.

One of the first calls I made after signing was to Sparky Anderson, who was now in his 15th season in Detroit. He was a smart enough manager, knowing when to stay out of front-office matters, but he was clearly pleased that I was back.

"We have the same rules?" I asked.

"Same rules," he said, and the conversation was as straight and as upbeat as anything we had known throughout our good years together.

I had no anxiety about returning to baseball. I knew I could play. I was in great shape, my hamstring problems were finally behind me, and the bat felt good.

I noticed as I arrived in Florida for spring training, and then back in Detroit, that club operations had changed during recent years. There had been improvements made to the spring training complex in Lakeland. We had a modern-day weight room and batting cage at Tiger Stadium, and travel and accommodations were better. The Ilitch organization was making it easier on families to be part of the picture, at home and on the road, and I liked the differences.

This team had been having its problems since our '80s heyday. Pretty much everybody was gone from that era, except for Alan Trammell and Lou Whitaker. Still, I didn't mind the thought of batting in the same lineup as Whitaker, Trammell, Cecil Fielder, Mickey Tettleton, Travis Fryman, and Tony Phillips. Things had gone well in spring training. We knew we were at least going to score runs—lots of them.

The great thing about opening day 1993 was that I was back in my home stadium, wearing the old Detroit "D", back home, where it all started, in front of my home town fans, which included my whole family.

The Tigers went from finishing eight games beneath .500 in

> **"I ALWAYS FELT GIBSON BELONGED IN DETROIT. LIKE SOME PLAYERS BELONG IN L.A., CINCINNATI, NEW YORK—GIBSON WAS DETROIT."**
>
> *—Sparky Anderson*

'92 to finishing eight games above in '93. Also, we had drawn nearly 2 million fans, which was about 500,000 more than the previous year.

I didn't tear it up—.261, 13 home runs, 62 ribbies—but the Tigers were satisfied that I had provided some fire and some leadership, and I was pleased that I had been able to play with my old fervor for an entire season, without once going on the disabled list.

I liked the new group of players, different as they were from the bunch I had known previously in Detroit. Travis Fryman, a kid who was developing into a quality third baseman, really impressed me.

Home again in 1993 after a 5-year hiatus.

Tony Phillips was, to a degree, like Fryman, in that he was a scrapping over-achiever. He had a huge impact on the lineup. Mickey Tettleton delighted me about as much as any guy I had ever known in Detroit. Tettleton was one of those guys who really studied opposing pitchers, picking up habits and signals that would give him an edge at the plate. We constantly compared information, which was not something you could do with many players.

Bill Gullickson was one of those down-and-dirty, give-me-the-ball, I-don't-care-what-happens guys teammates really appreciate. He was not shy about pitching inside, and he used that technique to its full advantage.

Mike Henneman was in another category altogether. He was not a stereotypical closer, not a relief pitcher who would come into the ninth inning and gas hitters, which probably frustrated a lot of fans, and to a degree, some of his teammates. He tended to make things exciting. And he carried himself in a confident way that probably rubbed a few people wrong. That's why I liked him.

What none of us could have anticipated at the start of the '94 season, though, was the beginning of a long strike barely past the mid-point of the season. The eight-month layoff that followed was a shame, primarily because it ruptured the relationship between baseball and its fans.

A great office to work in— Tiger Stadium.

We had stumbled to a 52–63 record, when the strike mercifully cut short our season. Ironically, it was proving to be one of my best years—in 98 games I had 23 homers, 72 runs batted in, and I was hitting .276. I only wish my personal stats had been able to prevent us from being stuck in last place in the American League East as we headed out the door for an ugly layoff.

I wasn't so sure, as the strike lingered into spring of 1995, that I hadn't played my last game. The Tigers had been silent about my returning to play again. I had decided to get on with life. My family and business concerns were enough to keep me more than busy, and I had tentatively booked a June fishing trip to Alaska.

Finally, in April, after strike talks heated up and an agreement was reached, I began to speak with the Tigers about a contract for 1995.

We were staring down the barrel of another midnight deadline. I had given the club a firm figure for the '95 season—$1.3 million. If I wasn't worth that to the Tigers, there would be no hard feelings.

I sat in my home, sipping from a bottle of nice wine, watching the clock tick away. Everyone with me—family and friends— thought I was crazy to play a contractual game of chicken when it seemed as if the Tigers could easily say good-bye.

At 11:55 p.m., the phone rang. It was the Tigers.

I said, "Guys, this is the number. Not a penny less."

We agreed, and we got ready for the abbreviated season.

The old energy was back.

There was a serious question whether Sparky would be back, and I admired the stance he had taken in spring training, refusing to manage replacement players who took our jobs when we were on strike. He was the only manager who took this stance. He stood up for the principles of the game, which is what he always taught his players.

But I didn't always agree with his decisions. Probably our biggest shoot-out during my second stint in Detroit occurred in '94, at home against the Yankees. They had a left-hander, Sterling Hitchcock, who in New York the week before had gotten me to 0 and 2 until I worked him for a walk. He was tipping his pitches, and by the end of the at-bat, I knew every pitch before it was coming.

A week later in Detroit, we were down a run with two out in the ninth and a man on second, and in came Hitchcock again, this time pitching to me with the game on the line. Sparky, unbelievably, decided to hit Eric Davis for me. Davis hit a fly ball to left for the final out.

Nothing Sparky Anderson had ever done crushed me as much. Nothing. I was so upset that on the way home I called JoAnn from the car phone.

I just kind of murmured to her, "I can't believe he did that."

"What?" She didn't know what I was talking about.

"He just pinch-hit for me in the situation I cherish most. I'm crushed. He couldn't have hurt me more."

I said nothing to Anderson for a couple of days, but the incident was working on me. Nonstop. Finally, I walked in, and I closed the door, which was the signal anything could be said.

"I just wanted you to know you hurt me worse than you ever have in my whole career," I said. "The fact that you took me out of a situation I relish, when you know there's nobody on this team who would rather have been up there. I don't believe it. I faced that guy in New York. I battled him for a walk. I had his pitches. And you put Eric Davis in there? He didn't deserve to be there. I deserved it. I don't know what the hell you were thinking about. Are you sure you're feeling OK?"

He was sitting behind his desk, listening to me completely, which was the way Anderson did things. He let you have your say. And I wasn't through having mine.

"Next time that situation comes up," I went on, "if you ever do that again, I'll rip your head off." And then I walked out.

Anderson was secure enough as a manager, and knew me well enough, to take such talk in stride. But I had made it a point throughout my career to have face-to-face conversations with my coaches and managers. Sometimes it was strong dialogue, though I doubt few athletes had better relationships through the years with their superiors.

It also worked the other way.

During that same '94 season, again in Detroit, I hit a pop-up that appeared to be foul. I barely jogged to first, the ball drifted back into play for the putout, and I had been caught in a glaring act of non-hustle. It was the only time in my career I had let something like that happen.

Sparky called me into his office afterward.

"I don't know what's going on with you," he said, "but that ain't you. I have never seen it, and I'm going to tell you right now, I'm never going to see it again. That ever happens again, and your ass will not be playing."

Fair to the bone—that was Sparky. He was right when he said an act as lackadaisical as my jaunt to first was not me. Truthfully, as I got into the '95 season, I began to realize how much about me had changed.

I wasn't the fury I had been in earlier years. I was talking more with opposing players. I was probably a gear lower in certain situations. I could still heat up—I hit five home runs during one week in May, including a big ninth-inning game-winner off Chicago's Roberto Hernandez—but the fire was fading. And I knew it.

It was becoming difficult to motivate and prepare myself, miles from the "taking no prisoners" stance of before. My body hurt more now that I was pushing 40, and I found myself less and less able to travel and to be away from my family with the ease I had once known.

Family, in particular, was making me less concerned about baseball, and more committed to having years together with my wife and kids—years that I knew would pass too rapidly.

Motivation became more of a problem when—before the August 1 trading deadline—the Tigers dealt two of our top pitchers, David Wells and Mike Henneman. We were only a couple of games out of first place in the American League wild-card race, and now a club stuck on the future was throwing in the towel in 1995.

I knew it was time. If I wasn't going to play in Detroit I wouldn't play anywhere else.

It was always hard to accept defeat.

I played in my final major-league game on August 10th at Texas. During the entire game, I simply was not into what was happening. I had my final at-bat against the Rangers' left-handed reliever, Dennis Cook, and, appropriately, I struck out. I said to myself at the moment I went down, "You were humbled coming in, you're humbled going out. Perfect."

After the game, the first thing I did was walk into the club-house and call JoAnn.

"Are you ready for me to come home?"

"Are you serious?" she asked.

We had been talking a few times during the preceding weeks about retirement. My words to her were no shock. The finality of it all washed over us. It felt good.

"I'm going to do it."

JoAnn said, "I'll be here."

Next, I walked into Sparky Anderson's office, same as I had done so many times over the years, and closed the door. He looked up at me like, "Oh, boy. What is it now?"

"Skip, I just want you to know I just did that for the last time."

He looked at me with this bemused expression, checking to see if I might be joking.

Keeping my eyes open and on the target as my dad taught me.

I CAME INTO BASEBALL WITH A STRIKEOUT AND I WENT OUT WITH A STRIKEOUT. I CAME IN BEING HUMBLED AND I WENT OUT BEING HUMBLED.

HOPEFULLY I'LL BE REMEMBERED FOR MY STYLE OF AGGRESSIVE PLAY AND BEING A WINNER. I'VE GOT TWO WORLD CHAMPIONSHIPS AND THREE PENNANTS—AND THAT'S ALL I EVER CARED FOR AND ALL I EVER PLAYED FOR, TO BE A WORLD CHAMPION.

"I'm going home," I said to him. "It was a great run. I appreciate everything that we've had together through the years. We'll always be great friends. I'm asking you just one thing: that you don't say anything. You're the only person on the team who knows. I'm going to tell Tram and fly with you to Milwaukee. Then tomorrow I will get up at 6 a.m. and take the first flight home, and announce it later in the morning."

Sparky said, "No problem." He knew what was coming. He had sensed I was nearing a decision, that I felt it was time for me to be with my family.

I said, "Don't even try and talk me out of it."

"I'm not going to," he said, and he was grinning and holding up his hands. "I know where you're coming from."

I felt absolutely awesome as I showered, dressed, and boarded the team bus. I brought along a couple of cold beers and pulled into a seat next to Trammell. I offered him a brew, but he wasn't interested.

"What?" I said, laying it on. "You're not going to have a retirement drink with me?"

He just looked at me.

"Shhhhhhh! I really need to keep things hushed," I said. "Don't say anything. I'm done."

Trammell actually did not believe me. He kept after me, expecting me to say it was a joke, probably because we had been kidding about retirement in recent weeks around the batting cage. It was in Detroit, and I was talking to Trammell and a couple of others during batting practice: "If I hit a ball over the roof on this swing, I retire."

Three times I hit a ball onto the right-field roof, and each time it came bouncing back, missing making it all the way out by maybe a couple of feet. I think it was the Big Man telling Mr. Gibson his time in baseball was nearing the end.

I think that's why I felt such elation sitting next to Trammell, savoring the vision of a good life ahead, knowing that I had been traded back to my family.

My family—the best team I ever played for. From left to right, in front, Kevin and Kirk Robert, my wife JoAnn, Cameron and Colleen.

Kirk H. Gibson

In the spring of 1997, I can look back with even greater perspective on a 17 year major league career. It is amazing what athletics can teach you in life.

Now my days are filled with teaching my own Kids responsibility and accountability just as my parents have shown me. I enjoy giving back via charities, helping those who aren't as fortunate. Environmental issues are a concern and an area in which I hope to make a difference. I want to preserve for future generations all the opportunities afforded me throughout my life.

Thank you to everybody I've encountered: Family, coaches and fans for growth and development — even to those whom I've alienated and clearly have not impressed with some of my previous actions and words. I have done none of this by design but by mistake, simply proving I'm only human. I continue to learn from every bit of praise and, more importantly, from the criticisms.

I now ask you, what is your WORLD SERIES? Set your goals high. Visualize success.

Ignore the Beast!

Kirk Gibson

PHOTO CREDITS

Allsport: 78, 146 (top), 147, 148
    Jonathan Daniel: 151
    Otto Greule: 144
    Will Hart: xi, 124, 134, 135, back dust jacket flap (center)
    Mike Powell: 139, 140
    Rick Stewart: 143
AP/Wide World Photos: 54, 89, 130
Detroit Free Press: cover, i, 86, 98
Detroit News: 6, 8, 9, 56, 66, 70, 71, 77, 82, 104, 108 (both), 109, 154, 156
Detroit Tigers: 4, 73, 95, 153
    Joseph Arcure: xii, 152
    Clifton Boutelle: 72, 97
Dwight Cendrowski: 159, all memorabilia photos
Matthew Koukios: 91, 92
Los Angeles Dodgers: 78, 112, 113, 114, 115, 119, 121, 122, 124, 129, 133, front dust
    jacket flap (center), back dust jacket flap (top)
Los Angeles Times: 136-137
Michigan State University: 20, 21, 22, 27, 30, 32, 33, 37, 39 (top), 43, 47, 49, 57
Sporting News: 85
Sports Illustrated: 60, 104
    Jacqueline Duvoisim: 1, 7
    Bill Epperidge: 2, 61, 62
    Andy Hayt: 88 (top)
    John Iacono: 128, 160, back dust jacket flap (bottom)
    Heinz Kluetmeier: 126
    Ronald Modra: 88 (bottom), 105, 111, front dust jacket flap (top)
Chuck Solomon: 116, 127, 145, 157, front dust jacket flap (bottom)
UPI/Corbis-Bettman: 3, 64, 65, 68, 76, 90, 93, 99, 102, 106, 107, 110, 123, 146 (bottom)